"Lockhart-Rusch uses the rich metaphor of Double Dutch jump rope to highlight how the 'tightrope' of hegemonic culture and history can be woven together with the 'second rope' of womanist engagement to facilitate playful, faithful learning that is deeply transformative. Her book is full of concrete examples of womanist pedagogical practices that can be embodied in theological classrooms, as well as places of learning far beyond the academy. We need this book; it's an essential reminder that God comes to us in the work and play of the margins, showing up in ways that bring joyful fun and communal engagement into being."

—*Mary Hess*
Luther Seminary

"*Doing Theological Double Dutch* clearly establishes Lakisha Lockhart-Rusch as a leading young scholar in the international field of religious education. In this creative and courageous text, she brings together the liberating and humanizing potential of play with a powerful womanist pedagogy, all to break new ground for educating in faith that is emancipatory for all."

—*Thomas Groome*
Boston College

"Lakisha Lockhart-Rusch's book weaves together womanist wisdom for play meant to nourish educators everywhere. Lockhart-Rusch skillfully shows educators what healing and inclusive play looks and feels like for spiritual communities bold enough to try. She invites readers to appreciate play through a womanist lens in ways that will transform their movement in the world."

—*Christine Hong*
Columbia Theological Seminary

"Lockhart-Rusch invites readers of all ages, cultures, and backgrounds to experience womanist play that seeks liberation, hope, and joy for all. *Doing Theological Double Dutch* is a necessary read for educators and religious leaders who are seeing the violence and trauma in the world, and want to offer joy and love. A field-defining book that will shape your imagination about what is theologically possible for both the children in our community and your inner child."

—*Patrick B. Reyes*
Auburn Theological Seminary

"*Doing Theological Double Dutch* playfully expands our imaginations about how much more liberating and meaningful educating for faith could be if we engaged in womanish modes of play. These pages are brimming with hope for change, deep wisdom from womanist 'mothers,' and most of all big love for all humans who long to be seen."

—*Courtney Goto*
Boston University School of Theology

Doing Theological Double Dutch

A Womanist Pedagogy of Play

Lakisha R. Lockhart-Rusch

William B. Eerdmans Publishing Company
Grand Rapids, Michigan

Wm. B. Eerdmans Publishing Co.
2006 44th Street SE, Grand Rapids, MI 49508
www.eerdmans.com

Book design by Leah Luyk

Printed in the United States of America

31 30 29 28 27 26 25   1 2 3 4 5 6 7

ISBN 978-0-8028-8373-5

Library of Congress Cataloging-in-Publication Data

A catalog record for this book is available from the Library of Congress.

Unless otherwise indicated, Scripture quotations are from the New
Revised Standard Version Updated Edition (NRSVue).

This book is dedicated to those who paved the way so that I could play and write this, to those who understand and find the Divine in creative, silly, and fun places: you too are deeply loved and made in the image of the Divine. You were created by a creative creator to create. Never stop playing and being exactly who you are. I see you and play with you.

I also dedicate this, my first book, to my family and especially the three E's in my life: Eddie, Edward, and Ezra. All of your support, compassion, imagination, joy, playfulness, and love made this book possible. Thank you and I love you three *con todo mi corazón*.

Contents

Part 4: Twenty Questions: Are We Doing Double Dutch Yet?

Foreword

The Black woman's body, the academic-Black woman's body, the academic-theologian-Black woman's body needs to play so that she may live, so that she may thrive. As I read *Doing Theological Double Dutch: A Womanist Pedagogy of Play*, Dr. Lakisha Lockhart-Rusch helped me remember when I as a fledgling Black womanist scholar didn't know how to play so that my Black body could live. I allowed my ears to hear only the White supremacist dominant voices in the theological academia that said, "If you don't publish you will perish!" My body stressed and strained from the physical and psychological burden of trying to jump the "tightrope" that seemed to be the only option in theological education. Yes, there were a few moments when I resisted the formula for academic success that was imposed on me if I wanted tenure and promotion: "Write for the audience that will review your tenure and promotion dossier," they said. I rejected that death sentence, but I still struggled to find true joy in teaching and writing until one beautiful evening I caught a glimpse of womanish play.

It was one evening after a very long day of back-to-back two- and three-hour sessions at the American Academy of Religion and Society of Biblical Literature (AAR/SBL) meeting in November 1996 when I and my roommate, Nancy Lynne Westfield, PhD, were sitting in our New Orleans hotel room. She opened this large notebook filled with poetry that she had written over the years and asked if she could read some of her work to me. I welcomed her undisclosed talent. With each reading of a different poem the muscles in my neck and back seemed to unwind and my legs and arms relaxed. With the reading of each poem, the smile on my face progressed from polite laughter to uncontrollable deep belly laughter. Of all her wonderful poetry it was her poem "Come Straight Home" that had me rolling from my bed to the floor. I still ask for that poem, on demand, when we spend time together at a conference and sometimes even during our phone conversations. That was one moment, among many, in our history that Dr. Westfield encouraged me to play.

Dr. Lockhart-Rusch reveals that what I was experiencing during our private poetry slam at AAR/SBL was a "womanish mode of play." She argues that such practices can "untether our identities" from dominant White supremacist heteronormative cis-gendered male and cis-gendered female authorities in theological education. When we engage in womanish modes of play, we practice critical consciousness and critical remembering of who we are as well as affirm the communities that fostered/formed our identity. This insight is just one of many ways Dr. Lockhart-Rusch has helped me name some of my experiences after twenty-six years in the theological academy.

Doing Theological Double Dutch uses the metaphor of double Dutch jump rope to expose the problem of theological education based on the mind-body dualism advanced by a White supremacist ideology. Dr. Lockhart-Rusch argues that womanism adds another rope of Black lived experiences and embodied realities to the single "tightrope" to make theological education more hospitable to all who seek to learn through embodied teaching and learning.

Methodologically, Dr. Lockhart-Rusch frames her book by placing Alice Walker's four-part definition of "womanist" in conversation with theories that include Black liberation and womanist scholars. She deconstructs the faulty idea of bifurcated bodies and minds in theological education and constructs instead her theory of a womanist pedagogy. Bodies and minds are woven together as they were created to be when we teach/learn and engage in practices that facilitate and celebrate our whole bodies. Theological educators must take note that we maximize wholesome learning that yields wholesome leadership in communities, congregations, and denominational judicatories when teachers'/learners' heads and hearts in one body are nurtured, when teachers/learners use their senses in "childish" play, and when teachers/learners acknowledge and affirm their communities and cultures in the process. Her book is filled with theory balanced by practice—womanish modes of play. Readers are gifted with practices meticulously detailed, followed by questions for reflection after each part of the womanist definition. Dancing, be it private or public, is one womanist mode of play that continues to help me become whole.

During the summer of 2005, Dr. Emilie Townes extended an invitation to womanist scholars from all disciplines to join her on a trip to Salvador, Bahai, Brazil. Dr. Stephanie Mitchem (theology and ethics), Dr. Yolanda Smith (Christian religious education), and I were the three scholars who joined Dr. Townes. For almost a month we enjoyed the beauty of the people, their culture, their stories, their food, and their religion. One afternoon while we visited a youth organization, the teens performed traditional dances. Following their performance, we were invited to dance. While I was reluctant, Dr. Smith did not hesitate to dance with the teens. She amazed us all with her graceful arms swirling and long legs leaping to the sound of the music. It was clear that dancing was Dr. Smith's love language. The teens' cheering, the music, and Dr. Smith's graceful movements encouraged me to move beyond just chair dancing to join her on the dance floor. At first, I felt awkward and out of place. However, the chanting encouragement of the teens and mirroring of Dr. Smith's movements assuaged my fears and propelled me to dance freely. I discovered that public dancing to unfamiliar music was playing. That time of public dancing was a moment of transcendence, where my spirit connected with the community, culture, and my ancestors cheering me on.

As I reflect on that time of public dancing, Dr. Lockhart-Rusch and her theory/practice of a womanist pedagogy of play have helped me realize the liberative power of dancing as a womanish mode of play. I also believe that Dr. Yolanda Smith, the preeminent womanist Christian religious educator and dancer who has transitioned too soon, is now dancing with our cloud of witnesses and cheering us on, encouraging all womanists whose lives she touched to dance, dance, dance!

Thank you, Dr. Lockhart-Rusch, for writing *Doing Theological Double Dutch: A Womanist Pedagogy of Play*. Your book is essential reading for theological educators who are serious about the future of theological education and its ability to prepare leaders as human beings that must have the humanizing aspects of play to be whole and healthy leaders. I look forward to the day that we go line-dancing. I am practicing so that I can publicly Wobble with you.

Evelyn L. Parker, PhD

Introduction

Being playful and playing are part of who we are as human beings. Think back for a moment to when you were a child. Think about when you played with other children. Did their skin color matter? Did their hair texture matter? Did their cultural upbringing matter? Did their religious affiliation matter? No. We all just saw another person to play with. We didn't place all of our baggage, stereotypes, or societal conditioning on our play partners. No, we saw them for who they were and we played.

As we played, we learned new things about ourselves and our partners. We learned to play fair and to be kind. We developed cognitive skills and agency as we made decisions. We learned to cultivate relationships and how to deal with things we were feeling inside. We made meaning of the world through our play. We gladly played across differences and were made better for it.

Even as adults, play remains important to our cognitive and affective well-being, meaning making, and capacity for relationships. I would assert that it's even more important for adults as we encounter racism, sexism, ableism, and ageism, as well as homo/transphobia, and other issues that challenge a person's worth, dignity, and well-being. Play empowers people in the face of oppression, interrupts and allows for reflection, teaches skills needed for living, and provides space for a creative and imaginative outlet to express, explore, and try things out. Play recalls us not only to our humanity and the humanity of others but also to our embodied realities.

I believe that this embodied play is not only part of our Christian story but also that it brings us closer to the Divine. Just look at

Scripture; it is chock-full of play. When I read the Bible, I often find myself cackling. Have you ever heard of a talking donkey? Me neither, except in Scripture. The fact that Balaam had not only a talking donkey but a *sassy* one who told him the truth and who saved his life is both amazing and hilariously playful (Num. 22). The act of creation is itself incredibly playful (Gen. 1-2). Just picture making grass and sky, night and day, flying things (birds) and crawling things (ants), and wild things (giraffes) and swimming things (like a clown fish)! How can one not see the play in that? There is plenty of dancing and singing too. One of my all-time favorite moments of play in the Bible is when Jesus is talking about the temple tax with Peter and essentially tells him to pay the tax collectors with money out of the mouth of a fish (Matt. 17:24-27). Ha! Can you imagine paying the IRS with money that you get from the mouth of a fish? I find God and Jesus to be very loving and playful. If we are seeking to be more like Jesus, then we too should remember our embodied playful selves—especially in theological education.

I was taught that theological education is an endeavor of the mind filled with theories and critical thinking, never mind the "very good-looking bag of bones" that I was carrying around to do all the thinking.[1] I found this demeaning and wrongheaded. Why is it that my Black woman's body could be objectified, gawked at, and commented on in classes and churches, but my mind didn't have its own insight to add to the conversation? How could I not bring my Black woman's body into the work that I felt that the Divine was calling me to do? Having higher regard for the mind than the body is not an anomaly within the academy. Mind over body thinking happens in classrooms, churches, homes, and organizations in the United States and around the globe.

This mind over body dualism is what I see as part of the problem within theological education. This dualism does not acknowledge the epistemology of the body, which is often the ontological reality of those in non-White and non-male identifying bodies. This dualism often leads to misogyny, racism, ableism, ageism, and homo/

---

1. This was said to me by a male professor in reference to my body.

transphobia. In theological education this dualism then shows up as a lack of diversity among leadership, staff, faculty, and students. It continues through lack of diversity and embodied resources on syllabi, in course planning and preparation, and in pedagogical methods and strategies, leaving many students struggling to understand how they live out a call in the world without their God-given bodies. How are students to reconcile the incarnational and fleshly reality of Christ, if they cannot embrace their own flesh? It is a contradiction that leaves many fragmented, hurt, and disillusioned by the church and theological education.

In her work, bell hooks speaks of an engaged pedagogy that bridges mind and body as well as teacher and student.[2] I will go a step further and say that her engaged pedagogy is also embodied as it requires recognition of both the bodies of the teacher and the student. She illustrates how some professors use the classroom as an opportunity to enforce their dominance over their students and strongly resist the idea of holistically incorporating one's mind, body, and spirit in the learning process.[3] I find this exercise of control and power in the classroom and resistance to holistic learning to still be true in much of theological education today. And hooks asserts, and I agree, that to educate for freedom and transformation one must not only incorporate the mind but the body and spirit as well. There must be a break from the traditional role of the professor valuing the mind and intellect over bodily experiences and knowing as they act as the sole bearer of knowledge with students being mere receptacles.[4]

We must make more space for the many ways in which people come to know, learn, make meaning, and have their being. We need to embrace more diverse means of teaching and learning in the classroom. This diversity can happen when we encounter voices and experiences that are not our own. When we encounter marginalized and

2. bell hooks, *Teaching to Transgress: Education as the Practice of Freedom* (New York: Routledge, 1994), 18.

3. hooks, *Teaching to Transgress*, 18.

4. Here I am referencing what Paulo Freire (in *Pedagogy of the Oppressed*, trans. Myra Bergman Ramos [New York: Continuum, 2005], chapter 2) calls the banking method.

oppressed voices and experiences, like that of Black women, we can begin to rethink how we know things and the many ways in which people come to know things. People not only learn and know through reading and using their minds but also through engaging their bodies and recalling lived experiences as well.

We must use our classrooms as places to resist and push back against the mind/body and student/teacher dualisms that have been the norm.[5] We should invite and welcome a more holistic learning and knowing experience that will deconstruct and de-center the kyriarchal epistemologies that reinforce domination, oppression, and submission.[6] This will in turn re-center more diverse and holistic epistemologies, experiences, and voices that are life-giving as they provide opportunity, agency, authenticity, freedom, and transformation.[7]

One medium through which to welcome these diverse ways of knowing is to take notice of and engage the body in the learning process in the classroom through womanish modes of play. A womanist[8] pedagogy of play can bring embodiment and engagement back to theological education and offers practical pedagogical tools for creating a clearing space to teach and learn across differences. This book looks specifically at the power of play, from a womanist perspective, within theological education. The need for play in theological education is great; it can aid in teaching and learning across difference through inviting persons to critically remember and reflect, deliberately question, creatively and collaboratively imagine, and fully live into emancipatory hope. This critical consciousness stems from and is deepened by womanist thought's invitation to embrace self, engage in culture and community, embody God's love, and to enkindle the world.

---

5. hooks, *Teaching to Transgress*, 21.

6. "Kyriarchal" is a term coined by Elisabeth Schüssler Fiorenza that recognizes overlapping layers of power. This term extends patriarchy to include other structures of oppression and privilege, such as ableism, racism, capitalism, etc.

7. hooks, *Teaching to Transgress*, 29.

8. I define the terms "womanish" and "womanist" in the following section.

Two Ropes

Double Dutch is a game that I played in my childhood. It incorporates two jump ropes that are turned by two people on opposite ends and in opposite directions while one or more players jump in the middle. It took me a long time to learn how to double Dutch. There were lots of falls and bruises involved, but once I got it, I was unstoppable. Doing double Dutch was incredibly exhausting and exhilarating all at once. It required focus to jump two ropes, to communicate with the rope turners, and to find a rhythm to sustain the jumping. Regardless of the hard work involved, I did it. I did it, and after doing it, I could do it again and again, and I knew I had accomplished something difficult in community, with my friends.

In this book I use double Dutch as a metaphor to describe my hope for theological education. In the pages that follow I explain the first single rope, which is a historical narrative that is told and considered most valuable—that of the life and experience of the White, cisgender, heteronormative male Christian. I call this rope the "tightrope." I then proceed to explain how adding the additional rope called "womanism" allows for a more expansive and inclusive understanding of this historical narrative and provides a possibility for moving forward by doing double Dutch together.

While there could be various other second ropes added to expand the narrative, I believe womanism is helpful in considering both our lived experiences and embodied realities. I believe this additional rope can make theological education a more holistic environment through embodied teaching and learning.

As we explore the need for this second rope it becomes critical to understand what womanism is. Womanism is often likened to feminism. However, womanism emerged because second-wave feminism did not adequately recognize and incorporate the experiences and histories of Black women or other minoritized women. Womanism is a theory and practice that celebrates and affirms the personhood, experience, and culture of Black women.

In celebrating Black women, womanism seeks to disrupt systems that silence and oppress not only Black women's voices and experiences but also all oppressed voices and experiences. Womanism realizes and uplifts the intersectional realities of class, race, and gender in which Black women—like many others—live and make meaning. The term "womanist" is attributed to poet and author Alice Walker. In her book *In Search of Our Mothers' Gardens*, Walker offers a four-part definition of what a womanist is:

1. From womanish (Opp. of "girlish," i.e., frivolous, irresponsible, not serious.) A black feminist or feminist of color. From the black folk expression of mothers to female children, "you acting womanish," i.e., like a woman. Usually referring to outrageous, audacious, courageous or *willful* behavior. Wanting to know more and in greater depth than is considered "good" for one. Interested in grown up doings. Acting grown up. Being grown up. Interchangeable with another black folk expression: "you trying to be grown." Responsible. In charge. *Serious.*

2. Also: A woman who loves other women, sexually and/or nonsexually. Appreciates and prefers women's culture, women's emotional flexibility (values tears as natural counterbalance of laughter) and women's strength. Sometimes loves individual men, sexually and/or nonsexually. Committed to survival and wholeness of entire people, male *and* female. Not a separatist, except periodically for health. Traditionally universalist, as in: "Mama, why are we brown, pink, and yellow, and our cousins are white, beige, and black?" Ans.: "Well, you know the colored race is just like a flower garden, with every color flower represented." Traditionally capable, as in: "Mama, I'm walking to Canada and I'm taking you and a bunch of other slaves with me." Reply: "It wouldn't be the first time."

3. Loves music. Loves dance. Loves the moon. *Loves* the Spirit. Loves love and food and roundness. Loves struggle. *Loves* the Folk. Loves herself. *Regardless.*

4. Womanist is to feminist as purple is to lavender.[9]

9. Alice Walker, *In Search of Our Mothers' Gardens: Womanist Prose* (New York: Harcourt, Brace, 1983), xi–xii. Emphasis original.

This definition has functioned as a starting point for womanist ethicists, exegetes, theologians, and scholars that we often continue to revisit. The first part of Walker's definition focuses on a womanist being "a black feminist or feminist of color" who is "acting grown up," "in charge," and "serious." This reflects the determination, leadership, focus, and perseverance that many Black women possess because of our historical realities and experiences.

The second part of Walker's definition sheds light on a womanist being a lover of women and women's strength as well as being "committed to survival and wholeness of entire people, male *and* female." This part highlights Black women's aspiration for community and deep desire for universal wholeness and flourishing regardless of difference. The third part focuses on what a womanist loves. It mentions how a womanist loves dancing and music, the moon and the spirit. . . . "*Regardless.*" An important piece of this third part is the notion of a womanist loving our very being, our culture, and the many ways we express our culture such as through dancing and music. Dancing and being musical are forms of play along with spades, double Dutch, and hand games. Here Walker is stating that part of being a womanist is to have love for the body and love for play.

The fourth part of Walker's definition provides insight into the relationship of womanist to feminist, which is analogous to the relationship that purple has to lavender. Womanism is not separate from feminism, but provides a more inclusive framework to engage race, class, and gender. Feminism exists within womanism just as purple is a vivid and dynamic color with a close relationship to lavender. They are both necessary, distinct, and coexistent.

Walker's definition offers language to what was already at play in the world, and has led to womanist theology, womanist ethics, and a womanist theological anthropology. From this definition came the work of the foremothers of womanist theology: Katie G. Cannon, Jacquelyn Grant, and Delores Williams. They laid the groundwork for me and all womanists who have come after them. They had to endure a great deal for me to even be writing this book today. It is on their shoulders and those of other great womanists that I stand and am forever grateful. It is with these foremothers in mind that I often use the term *womanish* alongside *womanist*. I use the term *womanist* to talk about the theology and social theory this book builds on, and I use *womanish* to describe modes of play informed by womanist theology but not exclusive to it. Just as womanism is not monolithic, neither is play, and *womanish* is a nod to that expansive reality.

Additionally, one of Walker's definitions of womanism above talks about a girl acting "womanish." It reads, "You acting womanish, i.e., like a woman. Usually referring to outrageous, audacious, courageous or *willful* behavior." I want to honor this aspect of womanism and invite courageous, audacious, outrageous womanish play.

A class with Dr. Amenti Sujai in my freshman year at Claflin University changed my life. We read Alice Walker, Patricia Hill Collins, Ntozake Shange, and Delores Williams. Until this class I thought something was wrong with me. But the moment I read Shange's choreopoem *For Colored Girls Who Have Considered Suicide: When the Rainbow Is Enuf* I finally felt seen and heard. I finally felt like my way of understanding the world through body and movement wasn't an anomaly, but cultural . . . womanish. I didn't know womanism existed, but the moment I experienced it I knew I was home. My feelings and thoughts finally made sense and I now had words to describe them. It was transformative and liberating. While this exact kind of experience is hard to duplicate, I do believe that womanism offers this kind of liberation for all who encounter it. By leaning into a specific experience, the universal is impacted and made better.

This womanist jump rope is integral to our cognitive and affective well-being and can be a valuable pedagogical resource for all theological education. Once this womanist rope turns together with the tightrope we can begin to use womanish modes of play as a pedagogical tool in our classrooms. Because while these womanish modes of play highlight the experiences and voices of black women, in so doing they highlight and uplift the voices and experiences of everyone. These modes of play remind us that this work is not done solely in the mind, but in the body as well. This rope advocates for an awareness and celebration of the cultural heritage and importance of the embodiment of Black women's playful identities. This rope promotes a sense of self and identity, of one's history and heritage, the value in community, and social action for the justice of God.

The Game Pieces

This book is presented in four parts that align with the four tenets of womanism. Each section contains four chapters and concludes with practical examples of womanish modes of play that can be implemented in the classroom. This book is written with an educator's eye for instructional design, which here means that each part builds on the last one and study can easily span a semester. Each part also contains both theory and practice and can stand alone as needed for a particular class or other unit of instruction.

The first part discusses two truths and a lie as it explores the context of our play—the historical reality of the United States, Christianity, and Black women's lived experiences—as it further develops the double Dutch metaphor. I engage the work of Willie Jennings, Henry Louis Gates Jr., and Charles Long to explain and raise issues of fragmentation and signification as well as colonial dominance and the prostitution of Christianity. I then look to the work of Emilie Townes and Katie G. Cannon to discuss both the historical reality of Black women's roles and stereotypes. Part 1 ends with practical examples of womanish modes of play that incorporate embracing self.

Part 2 deepens our understanding of womanism by looking at the work of Alice Walker, Stacey Floyd-Thomas, Eboni Marshall Turman, and M. Shawn Copeland. Using the work of these Black women I define womanism along with womanist theology, ethics, theological anthropology, and offer a womanist understanding of play as a cultural expression and experience. Digging into the incarnational connection to Christ and the need for ontological space for Black bodies, I argue that womanish play provides a clearing space that can be healing and rejuvenating and can be an act of radical resistance. Part 2 concludes with practical examples of womanish modes of play that incorporate engaging in culture and community.

Part 3 delves into play as a part of being human, expanding understanding of the many facets, characteristics, and functions of play. This part also discusses the mind and body connection, with a specific focus on the relationship between the kinesthetic and the neurological during play. Here I extend my personal definition of play as an embodied aesthetic experience. This part ends with practical examples of womanish modes of play that incorporate embodying God's love.

The fourth and final part of this book addresses important questions about the significance of a clearing space for a womanist pedagogy of play. Clearing space creates a place where flesh is acknowledged and one can be unashamed and free. And I make a case for the importance of clearing space by explaining how and why safe and brave spaces often fall short. I look to the work of Olivia Pearl Stokes, Anne Streaty Wimberly, Katie G. Cannon, and bell hooks for examples of justice and praxis walking hand in hand within womanist pedagogy. Part 4 concludes with practical examples of womanish modes of play that incorporate enkindling the world.

This book concludes with explaining that in embracing self, engaging culture and community, embodying God's love, and enkindling the world, a womanist pedagogy of play can transform the classroom into more holistic, diverse, and embodied spaces that support teaching, learning, and faith formation across differences.

The Rules

This book draws from relevant works in the areas of womanist theology and pedagogy, literature and ethics, history of African American religious and cultural experiences, social sciences, and play literature to assert that womanish modes of play can be a powerful and transformative resource in theological classrooms.

This book is rooted in and expands theoretical research, but each part also equips practitioners to implement a womanist pedagogy of play in classrooms by offering practical tools that aid in teaching across difference and enhance the role of the body in theological education. It's my hope that this work will set the stage for further exploration and research around womanish play as a pedagogical tool for adults as well as children in religious education.

It is important to note that these modes of play, while practiced by various other cultures, are distinct to African American women's culture and experiences and have specific meaning and significance to womanist's consciousness and ethics. My work highlights the importance of these modes of play from the perspective and experience of Black women and the benefits they can provide to all persons who engage in them.

Since this work is intended to speak to persons of all cultures, not just African American women, it is crucial to be aware of and avoid cultural appropriation when engaging in this work. By *cultural appropriation* I mean the point when borrowing or gleaning from another culture is not cited or referenced properly, or when borrowing/stealing becomes exploitative of that particular culture. In order to avoid this, I would encourage readers to (1) make sure you know who you are and why this speaks to you and your context; (2) do your own research about the culture and the practices outside of just books and articles—be with the people; (3) avoid stereotypes and things that are sacred and held close; (4) cite your sources, give credit, and amplify voices when you are inspired by thoughts, ideas, and practices; and (5) most importantly, be honest with yourself and others, actively listen and witness first, and be intentional in your actions.

This work is a cross-pollination of various disciplines. I envision you as theologians, religious educators, and students who are interested in bridging the Eurocentric mind/body dualism and want to make your classrooms more diverse, holistic places for embodied teaching, learning, knowing, and being. You are educators interested in using the various womanish modes of play as pedagogical resources in your classrooms to engender critical consciousness, reflection, and action individually and in community. While my particular interest is in the history, culture, and experience of Black women's play, this work has implications for all of those interested in embodied teaching and learning across diversity. It is my hope that this book helps you to live into a more diverse and holistic faith education that engages the mind, body, and imagination, as well as various theological aesthetics that help to connect people with the Christian story.

Theological education has the unique opportunity to highlight the potential of a womanist pedagogy of play as an embodied epistemology and ontological reality that is a celebration of cultural diversity, radical inclusivity, and liberative passion and excitement. Through womanist thought, values and convictions of the wholeness of a person and a community can be uplifted. It is through bringing these womanish modes of play into a theological classroom and curriculum that theologians can learn another way to educate the whole person in the love and grace of the divine, while cultivating community and caring for one's cognitive and affective well-being. In this context, a womanist pedagogy of play can become a prophetic practice that can remake theological classrooms by acknowledging the value in everyone's cultural experience of and with play. So, let's jump in together.

PART ONE

PART ONE

Two Truths and a Lie:

A Rope History

Chapter 1

The First Truth

In the United States and in the American academy there is a historical reality that all participants must recognize and understand: *there is one narrative that is told and considered most valuable—that of White, cisgender, heteronormative male Christians.* This is the first truth of this book. While this reality has affected many people and communities, I focus specifically on its impact among African American women. This truth and the worldview that it generates have allowed Black women's experiences, ways of knowing, and identities to be named and forced upon them by the dominant White male culture. This truth has created stereotypes, caricatures, and category boxes that Black women have been forced into. Dr. Emilie Townes identifies this truth as the "fantastic hegemonic imagination," which "helps to hold systematic, structural evil in place."[1] This is the false consciousness that there is only one way to view the world, and it is set by the dominant group.[2]

I liken this historical reality to jump rope.

In jump rope there is just one rope: often, there are three players, two hold each end of the rope and swing it in an arc while the third enters the space the arc generates and jumps or skips over the rope, careful not to stumble or trip. At other times, there is just one player, who holds each end of the rope and swings it over their own head and under their own feet. Most children jump rope for fun, but some play

1. Emilie M. Townes, *Womanist Ethics and the Cultural Production of Evil* (New York: Palgrave Macmillan, 2006), 21.
2. Townes, *Womanist Ethics*, 21.

the game for exercise. Success requires neuromuscular conditioning, skill at managing the centripetal and centrifugal forces of the swinging rope, a dynamic and acute sense of timing and rhythm. The danger of falling is real.

Our historical reality, like a jump rope, can easily cause one to stumble. Everyone is expected to be able to jump this first truth, but it is almost impossible to jump a rope swinging at a rhythm that does not account for the jumper's body type, ability level, environment (jumping space), experience (history of jumping), or culture (the how and why they might jump). The danger of tripping, falling, or getting hit by the rope are real.

How can one expect to engender change if the rope is designed only for a particular group, class, or set of jumpers? Theological education cannot expect to engender change across gender, race, sexuality, ability, and geography if the rope continues to turn by and for White male Christian scholars. Black women may attempt to jump this single rope, but we often fall, trip, or are injured by this rope in a game never intended for us. The rhythm of the single rope does not fit well with the reality of our lives.

As an undergraduate, I went to an Ivy League institution for a two-week long seminar on religion and philosophy. I was the only person of color and one of only two women in a group that included more than twenty White men. All the instructors were White men, and there was one in particular that I was very excited to meet since I was inspired by his work. I was eager to say the right things in the right ways to be accepted by him and the other professors at this seminar.

I thought things were going relatively well until the barbeque at the end of the seminar. The professor I admired made rounds giving everyone handshakes and thanking them for coming. But when he got to me, he stopped, patted me on the very top of my head like a dog, and said, "Well, at least you're attractive." Then he went on to shake hands with the White man next to me. I went to my room, locked my door, and cried. I cried with my fists clenched from a combination of frustration, sadness, and anger. I was frustrated that this professor I admired didn't see my potential, didn't see me. I was angry that he thought it was okay to not only belittle and demean me but to physically pat me on the top of my head. My entire body felt like it was on fire. First, my fists were clenched while I cried and paced around my room. The more I thought about why I even needed his approval to begin with I began to unclench my fists and to start shaking my hands out as if I were trying to dry wet hands that had just been washed. I continued moving around my room, but my pacing changed. I found myself moving more rhythmically. The more I allowed myself to be angry, the more I made it up in my mind that I would never allow something like this to happen to me again. Right leg, left leg, right foot pointed and right arm in a slow arc across my body and over my head. I would never again let someone hold this much power over me. I would never again allow someone to make me feel so small and insignificant. Both arms pushed out in front of my body then back into my body, hard and sharp, as my head, back, and entire body followed. No music, just the sounds of my crying as I began to dance. I had danced before, but this was the first time I danced out of anger and frustration. It was what my body knew how to do, so I did it. I danced until my body felt like mine again.

This was just one of the many instances throughout my own theological education that my Black womanhood was demeaned, considered less important and less valuable than my professor's White manhood. But this time the tightrope didn't just bruise me; it completely knocked me over, and it would take a year for me to get back up.

This historical tightrope is inherently oppressive and exclusive. While I would like to do away with this rope altogether sometimes, we cannot change history. As much as I wish we could, we cannot undo years of oppression and injustice. However, we can choose not to continue to turn this harmful and inequitable tightrope at the expense of others. Jumping with this tightrope has trained bodies and minds to both anticipate and fear things and has shaped our vision of the world and our capacities for pleasure in a certain way. This narrative alone is inadequate for living into our present reality and continuing into a future with a multitude of narratives, experiences, and voices. We need to introduce more perspectives if we're going to play together in a diverse society. We need an additional rope that contains multitudes.

Enter the womanist rope, one that uplifts the voices and experiences of Black women and in doing so also amplifies all persons who are oppressed and marginalized in the academy and society at large. Adding this additional rope of womanism expands our vision and increases the dynamic range and reach of our faith to other perspectives, abilities, genders, races, religions, epistemologies, and ontological realities.

Moreover, when the tightrope and womanism work together like the two ropes in double Dutch, rope jumping becomes an embodied communal activity that invites new ways of thinking about not only how to turn the ropes themselves but also how and when to jump. Doing double Dutch rejects the "divide and conquer" mentality and embraces a mindset that encourages wholeness, communication and understanding in community.[3] Adding an additional rope and learning how to do double Dutch and jump two ropes at the same time is very difficult, but it allows for double the reach, momentum, voices, and power of faith in community.

In order to jump these two ropes we must understand both the ropes and ourselves. In this process we might encounter what civil rights activist and historian W. E. B. Du Bois calls "double consciousness."[4] Double consciousness is the understanding and internal conflict of identity among subordinate groups who must live in an oppressive society and constantly see themselves through the lens of the dominant group. This experience forms part of the fantastic hegemonic imagination (mentioned above), allowing this type of consciousness and thinking to persist until an entire society believes that the dominant group is indeed in control and the subordinate group should be oppressed and viewed as less worthy, less human. The subordinate group must be aware not only of their oppressed mi-

---

3. Audre Lorde, *Sister Outsider: Essays and Speeches* (New York: Crossing, 1984), 112.

4. W. E. B. Du Bois, *The Souls of Black Folk*, 100th anniversary ed. (New York: Signet Classic, 1995), 45.

nority culture but their oppressed minority culture within the larger dominant culture—the White western male Christian culture. This makes understanding one's identity and reality a struggle twice over for the subordinate group. The addition of a womanist rope creates space for jumping between the cultures. The addition of a second rope involves more hands and voices, invites more challenge, requires more focus, and creates new ways of understanding, knowing, being, and jumping.

The tightrope is the narrative that is promulgated, most well-known, most often recited, and remembered. However, there are other narratives that should be told in order to understand minoritized voices and to appreciate why a second womanist rope is crucial. For, in fact, minority cultures are not to be the only groups who operate out of double consciousness. Everyone should understand the realities of oppressed cultures and the societies that oppress them. It is only by equally acknowledging the strength in difference that any country will have the power to begin to live in new and creative ways of being and acting together in the world.[5] To put it plainly, everyone can and should learn how to double Dutch!

I acknowledge the strength in difference by proposing creative new and imaginative ways of being and acting together in practical theology and theological education, while specifically concentrating on the realities of black people and, in particular, the realities of black women. For it is our mission that calls theological educators to create space for the kind of learning, growth, and risk that will set believers free through the transforming power of Christ.

5. Lorde, *Sister Outsider*, 111.

Chapter 2

The Second Truth

This brings us to the second truth about theological education: *there is a lack of diverse voices in theological education because of the historical realities of fragmentation and language.* In the United States, Black people's reality and place in the world has constantly been named for them through a discourse and language that is not their own. But Black women, both historically and contemporarily, have used various modalities in the process of conveying and creating meaning in order to generate a new narrative using rhetoric and language of their own. Through their various modalities, such as play, Black women rename themselves and their realities and embrace and embody ways of knowing and being.

Charles Long argues that signification is "one of the ways in which names are given to realities and peoples."[1] Further he claims, "the cultural reality of blacks in the United States has been created by those who have the power of cultural signification."[2] In other words, the White male culture has named Black people's reality and has represented the meaning of African American culture using their language and rhetoric, overlooking the capacity of Black people to name themselves and their cultural meanings.

Adding to Long's proposal, literary critic Henry Louis Gates Jr. defines signification as "the nature of the process of meaning-creation

---

1. Charles H. Long, *Significations: Signs, Symbols, and Images in the Interpretation of Religion* (Aurora, CO: Davis Group, 1995), 4.
2. Long, *Significations*, 8.

and its representation."[3] This refers to how people choose to represent another culture, person, or even themselves and can include undercutting gibes and subtle banter. Given the racialized and dominating history of the political and social interactions between Whites and Blacks, Gates distinguishes between significations and Significations. Although these words may seem the same, they come from two different discourses. The word *signification*, with a lowercase s, represents what White signifiers within a White discourse do; and the word *Significations*, with a capital S, represents what Black signifiers within a Black vernacular discourse do. Gates explains their paradoxical relationship as the "difference inscribed within a relation of identity."[4]

Depending on one's history and identity the word can take on a different meaning. This issue of language and rhetoric becomes crucial in meaning making and considering both significations and Significations.

Gates explains that "to revise the received sign (quotient) literally accounted for in the relation represented by the *signified/signifier* at its most apparently denotative level is to critique the nature of (white) meaning itself, to challenge through a literal critique of the sign the meaning of meaning."[5] Here Gates claims that White people originally signified or proffered a White representation of blackness in which, to be Black meant to be enslaved and considered less than White people. Because of this signifying of Black people's subjugated and oppressive reality, in naming ourselves, Black people had to revise what had already been signified about being Black. White representation of Blacks as enslaved and oppressed people became a kind of "colonizing trick" even for Black people, and White-devised rhetoric and formal language was deemed the only correct or appropriate way to signify Black people.[6] Black people were forced to learn how to jump the tightrope.

3. Henry Louis Gates Jr., *The Signifying Monkey: A Theory of African-American Literary Criticism* (New York: Oxford University Press, 1988), 47.

4. Gates, *Signifying Monkey*, 45.

5. Gates, *Signifying Monkey*, 47.

6. See David Kazanjian, *The Colonizing Trick: National Culture and Imperial Citizenship in Early America* (Minneapolis: University of Minnesota Press, 2003).

Since law disallowed reading and education for most enslaved people, they were often unable to fully learn formal English. Moreover,
they came from places within the continent of Africa and already
possessed languages, cultures, and communication systems of their
own. Since language and rhetoric signified a certain level of class difference between the races, Gates argues that Blacks had to engage in
a renaming ritual to "revise the received sign" and name their own
reality. Yet, to try to rename their realities for themselves, Black people had to use the "master's tools"[7] of formal language to Signify their
own meanings and sense of being.

We start to see how Black people were already placed in a disad-
vantaged situation in which their own languages and means of communication were not valued and their very identity and place in society was forced upon them. Black people were being forced to jump
a rope that was never meant or measured for them. This tightrope
turned at a speed/rhythm that was ingrained in White folks from
birth. One of the invisible privileges of growing up in the majority is
that it appears like you are skilled at something when in fact the thing
is just pre-calibrated to your experience and very existence. Here in
the United States, the rope is premeasured and turning at speeds cal-
ibrated to White specifications so there is no need for White people
to adjust or to worry about being hit by the rope. The tightrope was
literally created for White folks.

In contrast, Black folks in the United States today must still jump
this tightrope that doesn't fit our bodies or cultural rhythms. We have
to jump this rope that is too small, forcing us to shrink ourselves, to
trip and fall, or to be deeply hurt from the weight of the rope hitting

7. Audre Lorde, *Sister Outsider: Essays and Speeches* (New York: Crossing,
1984), 112. "Master's tools" is a phrase used by Audre Lorde in her 1983 article to
talk about the barriers of difference and what is deemed appropriate that are often
against minorities and their experiences. Her famous quote is "For the master's
tools will never dismantle the master's house." Here she is saying that we should
embrace our own differences and not try to do what the dominant group says we
should do because it will never change or deconstruct the systems of patriarchy,
hierarchy, or oppression; only using our skills and differences will do that.

us, all while being told who we are and that there is no problem with the rope, but with us, the jumpers.

A similar situation plays out in the academy. The rules and codes of the academy were made and set by a dominant, White, male group and culture, without consideration of the ways of knowing, communication systems, or identities of other cultures or groups of people. Therefore, when these "others" attempt to navigate or jump the ropes of the academy, the jumping is two or three times more difficult and discouraging. This tightrope was never intended for us and does not value our identity, our ways of knowing, or our communication and meaning making.

The work of womanist scholars Emilie M. Townes, Katie G. Cannon, and Delores Williams shed light on the realities of the historical roles, significations, and stereotypes of Black women. Due to the signifying of Black women and our cultural realities, Black women have employed various avenues of agency and formation to know and express ourselves outside of the framework designed and signified by the dominant group. Black women use our agency to rename ourselves for ourselves, and to tell a new narrative distinct from the ones that have been forced upon us.

The fantastic hegemonic imagination became a worldview that allowed for the signifying of Black women's realities as well as our ways of knowing and identities to be named and forced upon us by the dominant White male culture. This same fantastic hegemonic imagination became so pervasive that it allowed for the creation of stereotypes and caricatures of the categories that Black women were forced into.

As was briefly mentioned earlier, Emilie M. Townes introduces the infamous "fantastic hegemonic imagination," her term for the false consciousness that there is only one way in which to view the world, which is set by the dominant group.[8] The fantastic hegemonic imagination uses a "politicized sense of history and memory to cre-

---

8. Emilie M. Townes, *Womanist Ethics and the Cultural Production of Evil* (New York: Palgrave Macmillan, 2006), 21. Hereafter, references to this source will appear in the text.

ate and shape its worldview. It sets in motion whirlwinds of images used in the cultural production of evil" (Townes, 21). Images and roles that have been forced on Black women include the Mammy/Aunt Jemima, Tragic Mulatto, Welfare Queen, Sapphire, Pickaninny, and Black surrogates.

In looking at Black surrogates, we understand that the Black woman's body has been, and often continues to be, coerced, abused, and hypersexualized, often being viewed as chattel and commodified. During the antebellum period Black women served as surrogates while fighting for survival and quality of life. Black women had two kinds of social roles of surrogacy that affected them negatively: "coerced surrogacy and voluntary surrogacy."[9] The coerced surrogacy "was a condition in which people and systems more powerful than black people forced black women to function in roles that ordinarily would have been filled by someone else."[10] Black women were forced into roles of being sexual objects to White slave owners and serving as mammies to White families.[11] Their bodies, lives, and decisions were not their own and they were often forced to act as a substitute for White women in the home and in the bed.

Black women knew the experience of coerced surrogacy, and following emancipation, Black women had to uplift their Black men through voluntary surrogacy. This type of surrogacy came from the social pressures involved in "choosing to substitute their energy and power for male energy and power in the area of farm labor."[12] While coerced surrogacy was by force, this voluntary surrogacy was one in which Black women "chose" to act as a substitute for their Black men. Neither of these types of surrogacy was desirable or even fair, but it was a reality of life for Black women.

These were just the beginning of the various roles that were placed upon Black women and their bodies. Townes lifts up several

9. Delores Williams, *Sisters in the Wilderness: The Challenge of Womanist God-Talk* (Maryknoll, NY: Orbis Books, 1993), 60.

10. Williams, *Sisters in the Wilderness*, 60.

11. Marcia Y. Riggs, *Awake, Arise, and Act: A Womanist Call for Black Liberation* (Cleveland: Pilgrim Press, 1994), 48.

12. Williams, *Sisters in the Wilderness*, 73.

other images that have turned into caricatures and stereotypes that still exist today. Some images and roles that Black women were and continue to be segregated into are Mammy/Aunt Jemima, Sapphire, Tragic Mulatto, Black Matriarch/Welfare Queen, and Topsy/Pickaninny. In order to show how far these caricatures and stereotypes have reached, I will use modern-day examples from various media to explain and unpack each role and how they have turned into caricatures over time.

The Aunt Jemima role, which stemmed from the Mammy role, was to show just how happy Black women were with their work and their enslavement. The Mammy figure was "asexual, fat, excellent cook, excellent housekeeper, self-sacrificing, and above all loyal to her family . . . so loyal that she neglected her own family" (Townes, 32). She was often viewed as a "surrogate mother," caring for and nurturing White children, taking away time and energy from providing this same care and nurturing to her biological children.[13] Aunt Jemima was placed on boxes of pancake mix and bottles of syrup with a handkerchief on her head. This was one of many ways in which Black women's image, body, and skills were signified, bought, and sold. This role is one in which she possesses little to no sexuality, often seen as genderless and a hard worker (Townes, 48). Her cleaning is impeccable, her meals are delicious, and she is everyone's loving, compassionate mother figure.

This role is played out in modern-day TV shows when there is a heavy set, non-threatening black woman who mothers everyone. A modern-day example of this is the Miranda Bailey character on the TV show *Grey's Anatomy*. Bailey is a surgeon who everyone looks up to, is non-threatening, and holds everyone accountable. Everyone comes to her for advice, and she often has to choose between her job and her personal life. Bailey is not seen as someone desirable with a personal life until around season 6. She gets overlooked for awards and promotion while she is constantly sacrificing herself, her wellness, and her position to care for others in the hospital as witnessed by the fact that she does not become Chief until season 12.

13. Riggs, *Awake, Arise, and Act*, 49.

In contrast to the mammy, the Sapphire role is "malicious, vicious, bitchy, loud, bawdy, domineering, and emasculating . . . inherently and inescapably evil" (Townes, 61). This role is one that always makes the Black woman out to be bad, wrong, and nefarious. It is this stereotype and caricature that make it almost impossible for Black women to express themselves passionately or be assertive or decisive for fear of being automatically thrown into the angry Black women category. The modern-day Sapphire would be the character Annalise Keating from the TV show *How to Get Away with Murder*. Keating is a no-nonsense lawyer who doesn't take no for an answer and holds no punches in the courtroom or in life. She has no problem raising her voice and making her opinion known, even if it's at the expense of someone else's feelings. She is often referred to as a bitch or another angry Black woman because of her actions. She is rough and tough and seen as emasculating because of her assertive and blunt nature.

The Tragic Mulatto appears in two ways. First as "the light-skinned woman of mixed race . . . beautiful, virtuous and possesses all the graces of White middle-class true womanhood" (Townes, 85). Second as "a woman controlled almost completely by her libido," a harlot who breaks up homes, steals husbands, and nearly coerces the slaveholder to rape her.[14] The Tragic Mulatto is often seen as a desirable role because it is closer in skin color to being White than darker hued women. The closer to White the better, as they could sometimes "pass" or be seen as being White and be granted the preferential treatment and advantages reserved for White people. The tragic part is that this woman was often the victim of systemic and sexual violence. The modern-day tragic mulatto would be the character of Olivia Pope in the TV show *Scandal*. Pope is a light-brown-skinned Washington, DC, fixer. She falls in love with a White man who is not only married with children but is also the president of the United States. She is given status and privilege, as she is able to straddle two racial worlds. She is presented as untouchable as she rips

14. Riggs, *Awake, Arise, and Act*, 49.

apart a family and begins to find herself in a tangled web of power and control in which she delights.

It is also important to note that all three of these characters—Miranda Bailey, Annalise Keating, and Olivia Pope—appear in television shows created, written, or executive produced by one of the most powerful and influential Black women in show business today, Shonda Rhimes. Shonda Rhimes is a Black woman American television producer, author, and television and film writer, who has risen to the top in this industry.

I applaud Rhimes for her work and her success, and I also offer a critique. Through her work and some of her stereotypical images of Black women about whom she has written, developed, or executive produced, Rhimes has participated in the continuation of the fantastic hegemonic imagination. This is an example of what Long described when he mentioned how White culture signifies Black culture so much that Black folks begin to signify their own realities based on White folks' stereotypes and caricatures. Rhimes has been praised for creating shows with strong Black women characters and providing job opportunities for Black women actors. And at the same time, these roles continue to perpetuate the stereotypes that have been forced on Black women such as Mammy, Tragic Mulatto, and Aunt Jemima.

I think that Rhimes has done what she had to do to get into the industry, which is often the plight of the Black woman. She must "play the game" or "jump the rope" and become adjacent to privilege by giving people what they know and like in the form of stereotypes, until she has enough power to do things her way. This is, sadly, often how the system works for minoritized voices, especially for Black women.

The Black Matriarch, also known as the Welfare Queen, represented the "domineering female head of the Black family in the United States" (Townes, 115). She has many problems and is angry because she is a single mother with many children and must use welfare to support her family. This is often where the term "superwoman" comes from because the Black mother is forced to do and be everything for her family. Sometimes she does this well and sometimes she does not. A modern example of not doing this well would be the character Mary Jones in the movie *Precious*, based on the novel *Push* by Sapphire. Jones is the mother of her daughter Precious and survives off welfare, lives for her boyfriend, and uses her child as a servant to cook, clean, and sexually pleasure her whenever she wants.

The last image is the Topsy/Pickaninny who is "lazy, mischievous, wild-looking, and prone to thievery . . . nameless, shiftless clowns who were constantly running from alligators and toward fried chicken and watermelon" (Townes, 142–43). This role is seen to have little to no morals and to scare those around her. The modern-day Pickaninny would be the character Suzanne Warren, better known as "Crazy Eyes" in the Netflix series *Orange is the New Black*. Crazy Eyes is given her nickname because she acts crazy and offbeat. She lacks social skills and has emotional outbursts and obsessive tendencies, and everyone else is scared of her.

These various images were forced upon Black women and even many years later, these stereotypes and caricatures are still being played out in the media, for entertainment, just in different ways. This is how the world has come to know who Black women are and how Black women live and have meaning in the world. Black women are still constantly being placed into one of these categories, as evidenced by the ease with which one can find these images in popular media. While some of these images stem from a strand of reality, they are taken and contorted in a way that demeans and devalues the worth and very being of Black women. Townes says it best: "The damaging effect of such epistemological musings is that they take bits of Black reality and transform them into moral depravity as the norm for Black existence. This is structural evil working at its best (or worst). What this and the other stereotypes do is detract and deflect from examining the structures framing our existence and the assumptions we have made about the veracity of our knowledge about others and ourselves" (Townes, 116).

Through these images and roles, women's ways of making meaning and knowing, their bodies and their lives continue to not be their own. The experiences of these women went unseen as if all the suffering and pain they experienced were invisible (Townes, 149). Black women combat this fantastic hegemonic imagination and the various caricatures and stereotypes that have been mentioned through realizing that the story of Black women can be told another way.

The story of Black women is not only the story and images signified, given, and appropriated by White western male Christian culture. There is also a story of Black women that "can be told in such a way that the voices and lives of those who, traditionally and historically, have been left out are now heard with clarity and precision" (Townes, 7). There can be a story told of Black women that speaks to their compassion and care of all humanity, not just how well they cook and clean. There can be a story told of Black women's sense of morality, justice, and living for the good, not just what is deemed mean and assertive. These new narratives live and find meaning in womanist discourse. Womanist ethics, specifically, examines theories that concern action, relationship, and human agency while rejecting these social constructs that have oppressed and rendered invisible a group of women whose hard work and labor built this country.

The historical reality of the fantastic hegemonic imagination and signification have led to the fragmentation and the taking of language and culture of many minority populations, including Black women. This reality is just one of many that has led to a lack of diverse voices in theological education because of the many stereotypes and caricatures that were and are still perpetuated in our society. This reality not only affects minoritized populations but everyone, because if diverse voices are not present then there is still only one rope to jump. The same tightrope that does not consider the bodies jumping within it. The same tightrope that hits and hurts without apology. The same tightrope that was not measured or meant for anyone that was not White, male, heteronormative, cisgender, and Christian.

Chapter 3

The Lie

Gates poignantly questions: "What did/do black people signify in a society in which they were intentionally introduced as the subjugated?"[1] I would push this question further back and ask, Why were Black people intentionally introduced as subjugated to begin with? In response, Willie James Jennings asserts that one cannot discuss US history and identity without also discussing Christianity, without understanding critically how persons live, treat each other, and have their being in light of religion and the Divine.[2] Jennings states that there is "a history in which the Christian theological imagination was woven into processes of colonial dominance. Other people and their ways of life had to adapt, become fluid, even morph into the colonial order of things, and such a situation drew Christianity and its theologians inside habits of mind and life that internalized and normalized that order of things" (Jennings, 8).

Christianity's option for colonizing dominance has played a major role in the cultural formation and social construction of the United States. Christianity's use of the Bible as the word of God was used during slavery to keep human persons in chattel slavery. This repository of truth and wisdom provided comfort and hope for some and provided proof of racial domination and justification of violence for

---

1. Henry Louis Gates Jr., *The Signifying Monkey: A Theory of African-American Literary Criticism* (New York: Oxford University Press, 1988), 47.

2. Willie James Jennings, *The Christian Imagination: Theology and the Origins of Race* (New Haven: Yale University Press, 2010). Hereafter, references to this source will appear in the text.

others. As Jennings notes, "The intimacy that marks Christian history is a painful one, one in which the joining often meant oppression, violence, and death, if not of bodies then most certainly of ways of life, forms of language, and visions of the world" (Jennings, 9). Specific passages and translations of sacred Scripture were used to pacify the enslaved people, to keep them docile and frightened, while other passages were not allowed to be read to them. This shaping and fitting, subjugating the word of God to the system of chattel slavery, according to Jennings, explains why "Christianity in the Western world lives and moves within a diseased social imagination" (6). This leads us to the lie: *True Christianity condones, supports, or perpetuates oppressive treatment to any marginalized person or groups of persons.* This is not the Christianity that believes in the teachings of a historical Jesus who gave his life to save the poor, oppressed, and marginalized in this world. This is a lie.

Just as Long and Gates argued the importance and the effect of language and rhetoric, Jennings also asserts that through literacy, translation, and the vernacular, the dominant group made Christianity the vehicle through which they justified the displacement of other groups of people and regulated their identities through manipulating the Scriptures to affirm their unqualified primacy and privilege. This hierarchical system valued the commodification of place, space, and geography over and above genuine human relationships and community with diverse individuals and groups. We cannot face up to present social realities if we deny this history and "bypass the deeper realities of Western Christian sensibilities, identities, and habits of mind which continue to channel patterns of colonialist dominance" (Jennings, 8).

The kyriarchal history of the United States has systematically conditioned its inhabitants to know and understand who and what are important, to know and to understand to whom dignity and value must be accorded by way of external or empirical criteria grounded, among other things, in race, religion, class, gender, sexuality, and ability. In other words, through epistemology—how one comes to know—one either accepts and surrenders to oppressive signification or contests and repudiates it.

Asian feminist theologian Kwok Pui-lan rightly declares: "I have been reflecting on my long intellectual journey to 'struggle to know.' Why is knowing a struggle? It is a struggle because you must spend years learning what others told you is important to know, before you acquire the credentials and qualifications to say something about yourself. It is a struggle because you must first affirm that you have something important to say and that your experience counts."[3] Here Kwok is naming a reality for many women and other racial, ethnic, and cultural minorities. Non-White non-men in the United States have struggled to know ourselves because we have been told that we and our stories, our language, our means of communication and expression, our ways of knowing are not important, pertinent, or valid within the academy except as exotic objects of anthropological study. We are told repeatedly that our religion supports and affirms our oppression, enslavement, and servitude. Women and other minorities are told that other stories, experiences, languages, and ways of knowing are more important than ours. These other stories, experiences, languages, and ways of knowing must be engaged before studying or reflecting on our own. These continued patterns of colonial dominance and hegemony must be de-centered if Black women and all minoritized persons are to re-center and live into their full identities in the triune God of love, community, and justice revealed in Jesus Christ.

By using the lens of the lives and experiences of Black women, we can see, analyze, challenge, and resist all types of oppression while being a catalyst for change. This type of womanist thinking, knowing, and being exposes the injustices toward all marginalized persons and communities just as Jesus did.[4] This type of theological anthropology allows persons to view others and themselves in a more holistic way as beings made in the image of God. Not just the mind is

3. Kwok Pui-lan, *Postcolonial Imagination and Feminist Theology* (Louisville: Westminster John Knox, 2005), 29.
4. Cheryl A. Kirk-Duggan, "Signifying Love and Embodied Relationality: Toward a Womanist Theological Anthropology," in *Womanist and Black Feminist Responses to Tyler Perry's Productions*, ed. LeRhonda S. Manigault-Bryant, Tamura A. Lomax, and Carol B. Duncan (New York: Palgrave Macmillan, 2014), 43.

made in God's image, but the heart, body, and entirety of a person. Womanist theological anthropology looks not just to the individual but to the community, the culture, the life and experiences that we hold in the very marrow of our bones.

Jennings speaks eloquently about this diverse reality in relation to Christianity: "A Christianity born of such realities but historically formed to resist them has yielded a form of religious life that thwarts its deepest instincts of intimacy. That intimacy should by now have given Christians a faith that understands its own deep wisdom and power of joining, mixing, merging, and being changed by multiple ways of life to witness a God who surprises us by love of differences and draws us to new capacities to imagine their reconciliation" (Jennings, 9). Christianity is a religion that celebrates interconnected diversity and values differences. It is those in power who have resisted diversity and difference and prostituted Christianity for their own personal gain. There are a multitude of ways in which to live and have being, and a God of love, justice, freedom, and reconciliation values all.

While no group is monolithic, the history and continued oppression of non-White and non-male persons in the United States is real. The dominant group believed and acted as if anyone who did not look like them, speak and express meaning like them, or come to know like them was inferior. This fantastic hegemonic imagination continued to foster this belief and action in others, including the oppressed who began to believe and be convinced by the church, others in power, and political parties that they were in fact inferior. If a group or a person did not share the same skin color, gender identity, language, or religion they were suppressed and not seen as equals. Since the dominant group held the most power, this mindset and worldview became pervasive and has continued to permeate the minds and realities of those in the United States throughout the years.

Every person living in our society, with this history, has been conditioned as to how they come to know who they are and their place in the world based on the realities that have been named for them by the group in power. To state this more directly and personally, *we* have been conditioned on how we come to know who we are and our place in the world based on the realities that have been named for us by the White, cisgender, male Christian group in power. This dominant group used language, rhetoric, and religion to control, oppress, and fragment cultures and groups of people simply because of our differences. This is the historical reality that African American women were brought, bought, and born into. This is the historical reality that continues to run rampant in halls, classrooms, offices, and boardrooms of institutions of theological education. These are the truths that must be named, seen as discriminatory and oppressive, then disrupted and dismantled in order to effect change moving forward.

Chapter 4

Womanish Modes of Play

Embrace Self

Below is part one of the womanist definition and the accompanying ethical tenet of womanism from Alice Walker and Stacey Floyd-Thomas.

From womanish (Opp. of "girlish," i.e., frivolous, irresponsible, not serious.) A black feminist or feminist of color. From the black folk expression of mothers to female children, "you acting womanish," i.e., like a woman. Usually referring to outrageous, audacious, courageous or *willful* behavior. Wanting to know more and in greater depth than is considered "good" for one. Interested in grown up doings. Acting grown up. Being grown up. Interchangeable with another black folk expression: "you trying to be grown." Responsible. In charge. *Serious.*[1]

Like a girl child, a womanist is radical because she claims her agency and has a subjective view of the world in which she is not a victim of circumstance, but rather is a responsible, serious, and in-charge woman. Thus, the intergenerational lesson of radical subjectivity is to wrest one's sense of identity out of the hold of hegemonic normativity.[2]

---

1. Alice Walker, *In Search of Our Mothers' Gardens: Womanist Prose* (New York: Harcourt, Brace, 1983), xi–xii. Emphasis original.
2. Stacey Floyd-Thomas, *Mining the Motherlode: Methods in Womanist Ethics* (Cleveland: Pilgrim, 2006), 8.

Note the focus on the self and the actions, behaviors, and agency of self. The beginning step and nucleus of womanish modes of play is self-identity and claiming or reclaiming one's true self and agency in the world. It's imperative that the person begins with the authentic self. We must look within and evaluate, assess, deliberately question, and honestly examine and critique our motives, intentions, and biases to better understand where we currently are in order to learn, grow, and make the necessary changes to move forward. We are all products of our environment and have been conditioned in various ways by society—hence why play is a cultural expression whether we want it to be or not. Thus, everyone has some type of bias that needs to be acknowledged, questioned, and worked through. We must start inward in order to move outward into the world in an authentic way that is real and true to who we are, our context, our culture, and our community. While this is focusing on the personal self, this works similarly within a community. Together a community must evaluate, assess, and deliberately question where they are in order to plan and anticipate how and where they might grow and move into the future together.

In examining ourselves it is crucial to critically remember our history, heritage, and the happenings and persons that have led to our being in the space and place we are currently in. This includes asking hard consciousness-raising questions while looking at our heritage and ancestry in order to know and understand our lineage and hereditary patterns. It means taking seriously the two truths and the lie that was just discussed above. It means critically analyzing our complicity in the fantastic hegemonic imagination. It means realizing where we are leaning into and even using Black women stereotypes and caricatures. For a womanist, acknowledgment that we are here because of those who have come before us and because of the Divine is crucial. Therefore, in order for us to truly know ourselves, we must know and understand our history, culture, and predecessors, upon whose shoulders we stand, while also placing our own story and history within the Christian story. This applies similarly within a community. There must be research and a genealogy made from within the community. There needs to be critical remembering and conscious questioning about how and why the community came to be. Who was involved and why? Who had the power, who did not, and why? Who made the decisions and why? Who was left on the margins and why? Where is God moving in the midst? What are the truths and what are the lies?

These playful practices of embracing self involve going deeper and beyond what is already known to what is unknown and possibly even hidden or masked and asking what, why, how, when, where, and who was involved, all in the interest of coming into personal agency and freedom. These practices can be, but are not limited to, curating a creative selfie, dancing, playing twenty questions, and engaging an embodied autobiography.[3] An educator can utilize any of these to bring about introspection, self-discovery, and examination for individuals and for a community while having embodied aesthetic experiences and cultural expressions. These womanish modes of play invite students to get to know themselves, God, and those who have formed them into the persons they are while having fun, inviting humor, and allowing for improvisation. This includes both the good and the bad experiences as play not only holds space for joy and happiness but also for lament, grief, and rage. The educator can invite students to ask themselves and their families questions that invite them to critically remember and analyze; to dig deeper.

These modes of play can serve as fun and illuminating reminders of what each person brings with them into every space they enter and how others might be doing the same. These practices highlight the importance of knowing self in order to practice inclusivity and to reach out to the other. Just as we are all aware that we bring our stories with us, we need to make that same space for the stories and the bodies of the other. This might include making space for the need to re-story and begin to tell a new narrative that is more life-giving and emancipatory for self and others.

3. I use the term *embodied autobiography* to refer to an account of a person's life embodied and depicted by that person outside of just the written word. This may be accomplished through visual means such as art, theater, etc.

Essentials and Suggestions

Each womanish mode of play stems from a womanist consciousness, culture, and experience. These modes of play allow for students to remember, question, and claim their identity while exploring their heritage, their history, and the Christian story in order to further enrich who they and their communities are. They are also embodied aesthetic experiences and cultural expressions that are fun and require imagination while inviting possibility.

What embracing the self through conscious questioning and critical remembering does is allows us to see ourselves and this dominant narrative more objectively. When this happens, we are able to untether our identities from the one forced or placed upon us. It allows us to resist and push back against the fantastic hegemonic imagination that continues a dominant patriarchal narrative.

These self-embracing womanish modes of play bring about conscientization and emancipatory historiography. These practices encourage critical reflection and questioning about this country's history, the Christian story, and the realization and awareness that what is normative and what is true are not synonymous. When acknowledging these differences, one begins to acknowledge the various oppressions and injustices that are taking place. When people know more about where they have come from, they are better able to know and understand themselves and therefore claim their identity and agency in real, fun, and liberating ways personally and within their community. The following practices are examples of practical playful ways in which we can enact our agency as we come to a realization about the history of this country and our families/communities. We do this while also being agents of change in using creative and collaborative imagination to push forward a new narrative of liberation and hope.

The important key to these modes of play is for not only the educator to ask students conscious questions and to critically remember, but to encourage students to ask these things of the system, the educator, and each other. These questions and remembering should invite reflection about the social influences and dominant narratives that may have led to their ancestors or community being demeaned or discriminated against. This should be followed by a large conversation about those particular social influences and dominant narratives, how they came into existence and why. This also means the Biblical text and Scriptures are needed for reflection to aid in the understanding of God's liberating activity in the word and God's desire for liberation for all persons. The combination of reading Scripture and asking conscious questions playfully is vital so that persons can come to a place of conscientization where their histories can be emancipating.

Pedagogically, these self-embracing modes of play invite persons to start from within and critically reflect on one's own story in light of the Christian story. Then we can come to a new awareness or realization about God, our families, our communities, and ourselves. This will allow us a lens by which to see the world and ourselves to enact our own God-given agency in playful and liberative ways. This agency will empower us to bring awareness and understanding into our own communities, churches, and classrooms. These playful practices make space for both the power of radical subjectivity and social consciousness that rejects the normative and dominant narrative, not only with history, but also with self and the other. It allows for a more neutral ground on which to meet the other and begin to learn across differences so that we can see the other as they are and not as we might have previously thought or desired them to be.

Womanish Modes of Play: Embrace Self

- *Womanish mode of play:* Creative selfie.
- *Materials needed:* A mirror or the camera feature on a device, materials to depict oneself (e.g., paper and pencil, Legos, Play-Doh, clay, paint, etc.).
- *Environment/space:* A place with a flat surface to use for creating and possibly a table covering, depending on materials that will be used.
- *Directions:* After giving each student a mirror and creating materials, give them time to depict themselves, just as they see them-

selves. Give them time and space to really sit with who they are and how they want to depict that. After they have created their selfies, offer reflection space to discuss what they have depicted: Why have they depicted themselves as they have, and what does that depiction mean? Invite them to think deeply about what they see and who they are so they can truly embrace self.

- *Questions for reflection:*
  - What do you see?
  - How do you feel about what you see?
  - Is this who you are? Is this who you want to be?
  - What are three things you love about yourself?
  - What are three things you would like to change about yourself?
  - How has your history, ancestry, and past experiences shaped you into who you are?
  - Do you love yourself?
  - Do you feel deeply loved by the Divine and others?

- *Womanish mode of play:* Dancing.
- *Materials needed:* Music and a device on which to play the music (e.g., phone, computer, speakers, sound system, etc.).
- *Environment/space:* Open space for movement and privacy, if desired.
- *Directions:* Play the desired music and allow students to move and dance freely with no set moves or choreography. Allow space for students to embrace their own bodies and move as they feel. Curate space for students to sit with the awkwardness and fun to truly embrace self.
- *Questions for reflection:*
  - How often do you move your body freely?
  - What might be keeping you from moving your body freely?
  - How does your body feel when you are moving and dancing?
  - What might those sensations be telling you about your body?
  - Overall, how do you feel when you are moving and dancing and why?
  - What might it look like to make time for this every day, even for a short while?

- *Womanish mode of play:* twenty questions.
- *Materials needed:* No items are needed for the practice itself; however, one might desire to journal or record what is said. If recording is desired, a student might need materials to write and draw or a device for recording.
- *Environment/space:* Enough space for the persons to sit, stand, or move comfortably.
- *Directions:* In this practice, one person is the answerer and one or more persons can be the asker or askers. This can be done alone, in pairs or in groups around particular themes. The askers are to ask rapid fire questions and the answerer is to answer the questions equally as quick, without over-thinking, just answering the question as it comes. The askers are to ask fun, silly, reflective, and meaningful questions to continue to both embrace self and invite the other to embrace self.
- *Questions for reflection:*
    - For those answering questions:
        · What new information did you learn about yourself?
        · What surprised you most about your own responses?
        · What question(s) did you find yourself wanting to be asked and why?
        · How did the questions make you feel?
    - For those asking questions:
        · What questions did you ask and why?
        · What did you learn from the person(s) you questioned?
        · How did you feel asking the questions?
        · What questions do you want to be asked of you?

- *Womanish mode of play:* Embodied autobiography.
- *Materials needed:* Whatever materials the student(s) need to tell their story.
- *Environment/space:* Whatever space is needed for the students(s) to tell their story.
- *Directions:* Invite students to share their stories with themselves. Often, we move to inviting students to share with classmates, but they need to share with themselves first. Then as the class goes on

you can invite them to share in class, as they feel moved. No one owes anyone, professor or classmate, their story. Often, they need to see it and feel it for themselves first before they can invite others to bear witness to it. Invite it to be done with theatrics, improvisation, comedy, and various props—however they want to embody it. They can do this around a particular generative theme of their lives or chronologically. Curate space for them to be honest with who they are and their story in order to embrace self.

- Questions for reflection:
  - How did it feel to tell your story?
  - Why did you choose to tell your story this way?
  - As you were telling the story what did you feel?
  - As you were telling the story, were there things you wanted to adjust or change? If so, what were they and why did you want to change them?

Making a creative selfie, dancing, asking twenty questions, and telling an embodied autobiography are not new things or concepts. However, when we do these things with a playful womanist consciousness and understanding in mind, we become more intentional in our actions and care for ourselves and others. While curating a creative selfie might seem simple enough, when we put that into perspective around the lived realities of Black girls and women of abuse, oppression, suffering, rape, and constant bodily objectification, a creative selfie takes on new meaning. This selfie as well as the dancing become mediums of self-empowerment and embrace, of taking back agency of a body and self that have not always been our own.

The playful practice of asking twenty questions for Black women—when we were young girls—was one of the ways in which we were considered to be "being womanish" or grown-up, by learning more information than we might have needed to know—also known as being nosey. This practice can be revelatory about our history and heritage, and what we do and do not know. This playful practice invites persons to think more critically and reflect more spontaneously.

Finally, an embodied autobiography has particular significance for Black women as many of our stories have not been told. Stories have been told for, given to, or placed upon Black women. Having space to tell our own story or re-story as we desire to is a crucial way in which Black women enact and take back our agency in a world that has not deemed us or our stories as important. In this same vein it makes space for others to tell their stories as well.

The womanish modes of play offered here are but a few examples of playful ways in which one can practice radical subjectivity and begin to truly embrace self. Making this kind of space to embrace self is necessary and powerful not only for Black women but for others who have had similar or different experiences and need to reconnect with their own body, power, story, and agency. These womanish modes of play can be a pedagogical tool that leads to real transformation and liberation.

Practical Example of Embracing Self

While teaching a class, I wanted to give the students a chance to get to know themselves and each other before we embarked on our journey together. First, I invited them to tell their favorite biblical story or parable, the one that has stuck with them the most in life. I asked them to discuss why that parable stuck with them and what they felt it did for them in their lives. Some students just talked about the parable and others acted it out—it was hilarious and fun.

Second, I invited them to tell a story about a time when they were formed or educated in the Christian faith. I invited them to critically remember and reflect on their formation experience by giving them a list of consciousness-raising questions to consider. The list included questions about the form, structure, and process in which their faith formation happened; questions about whether the process was effective or ineffective; questions about who was present, who held power and authority and why; questions about the history that is known and why; and questions about the dominant narrative that is told, what it does to other narratives, and why.

Then as homework I invited them to do an embodied autobiography. I invited them to think about our class time and their own stories. I invited them to tell their stories to and for themselves in any way they desired.

At our next class many students were upset with me. They told me how difficult the assignment was and how this is not what they expected to be doing. They talked about how they realized new things about themselves, how they had never actually told their stories to and for themselves before and how empowering and sacred that felt. They talked about how it made them emotional in a way that they had not anticipated. Then, they began to share in class. I quickly reminded them that they were not required to share their stories in class, and that the assignment was just for them. They said they knew but wanted to share anyway. They talked about suffering and oppression, about God's moving in their lives, about lament and grief, and joy and love. It was beautiful to witness such embracing of self, often with humor, creativity, and imagination.

In that class we created clearing space for vulnerable sharing and truth telling. The sharing was followed by vital discussion and reflection on the similarities and differences in both the biblical stories shared before and in each other's embodied autobiographies. I invited them to ask more conscious questions of one another. This really got them involved and thinking critically about what formation and Christian education meant to them as well as the history and happenings that brought them to where they are. For some this included the parables mentioned and finding where their stories connected to the Christian story. This also aided in helping students get to know each other and some of their experiences, which was transformational for the classroom dynamic.

I found that there was much more discussion and asking of questions rather than micro and macro aggressions because they took the time to play and share together. Because of their playing together they were able to see the other, not just as a talking head with ideas, but as fully embodied persons with stories, histories, and experiences. They no longer had solely their own stereotypes, biases, or past experiences upon which to assess or attribute to a given person. Now, they had actual stories and experiences in which they could see and understand the other in new ways. With this knowledge, persons no longer had to rely on the dominant narrative since they now had a new narrative that was known in a real and embodied way.

Having a new narrative that resists the dominant oppressive and unjust narrative aids in all persons being able to see and understand the other in a way that allows everyone to learn across differences using more fun. The womanish mode of play of embodied autobiography with critical remembering allowed my students to embrace themselves and each other as part of the larger Christian narrative in new and liberating ways.

PART TWO

Mother, May I?
The Rope Jumpers
and Turners

Chapter 5
Who Is Mother?

As we explore the reality of Black women and play with a womanist understanding, it becomes critical to know and comprehend exactly what womanism is. While I explained and laid out the definition in the introduction, I will explain it once more in this chapter for emphasis. Womanism is often compared or likened to feminism, but we will remember that womanism emerged because second-wave feminism did not adequately address or include the experiences and histories of Black women or other minoritized women. Womanism is a theory and movement of practice that celebrates and affirms the personhood, experience, and culture of Black women. In celebrating Black women, womanism seeks to disrupt systems in place that silence and oppress not only Black women's voices and experiences, but all oppressed voices and experiences. Womanism uplifts the intersectional realities of class, race, and gender in which Black women—like many others—live and make meaning. This term is attributed to poet and author Alice Walker. In her book *In Search of Our Mothers' Garden*, Walker offers a four-part definition of what a womanist is:

1. From womanish (Opp. of "girlish," i.e., frivolous, irresponsible, not serious.) A black feminist or feminist of color. From the black folk expression of mothers to female children, "you acting womanish," i.e., like a woman. Usually referring to outrageous, audacious, courageous or willful behavior. Wanting to know more and in greater depth than is considered "good" for one. Interested in grown up doings. Acting grown up. Being grown up.

Interchangeable with another black folk expression: "you trying to be grown." Responsible. In charge. *Serious.*

2. Also: A woman who loves other women, sexually and/or nonsexually. Appreciates and prefers women's culture, women's emotional flexibility (values tears as natural counterbalance of laughter) and women's strength. Sometimes loves individual men, sexually and/or nonsexually. Committed to survival and wholeness of entire people, male and female. Not a separatist, except periodically for health. Traditionally universalist, as in: "Mama, why are we brown, pink, and yellow, and our cousins are white, beige, and black?" Ans.: "Well, you know the colored race is just like a flower garden, with every color flower represented." Traditionally capable, as in: "Mama, I'm walking to Canada and I'm taking you and a bunch of other slaves with me." Reply: "It wouldn't be the first time."

3. Loves music. Loves dance. Loves the moon. *Loves* the Spirit. Loves love and food and roundness. Loves struggle. *Loves* the Folk. Loves herself. *Regardless.*

4. Womanist is to feminist as purple is to lavender.[1]

This functions as a springboard for womanist scholars. The first part of Walker's definition focuses on what Floyd-Thomas calls "radical subjectivity"[2] or a womanist being "a black feminist or feminist of color" who is "acting grown up," "in charge," and "serious." I name this first part: *embrace self.* This reflects the determination, leadership, focus, and perseverance that many Black women possess because of their historical realities and experiences and the need to embrace all the parts of who they are that many must hide or make smaller. When the aforementioned characteristics are lived out by Black women, they are often labeled as bossy or bitchy. Many of the stereotypes and caricatures from chapter 2, such as Mammy and

1. Alice Walker, *In Search of Our Mothers' Gardens: Womanist Prose* (New York: Harcourt, Brace, 1983), xi–xii. Emphasis original.

2. Stacey M. Floyd-Thomas, *Mining the Motherlode: Methods in Womanist Ethics* (Cleveland: Pilgrim, 2006), 8.

Sapphire, come to mind here. This happens most often when these attributes of being "in charge" and "serious" are seen on their own and are not contextually placed within the experience and history of the lives of Black women.

The second part of Walker's definition, which Floyd-Thomas calls "traditional communalism,"[3] sheds light on a womanist being a lover of women and women's strength as well as being "committed to survival and wholeness of entire people, male and female." This part highlights black women's aspiration for community and deep desire for universal wholeness and flourishing. I name this part: *engage in community and culture* since that is what we do when we are striving for the wholeness and liberation of our people. The third part, which Floyd-Thomas calls "redemptive self-love,"[4] focuses on what womanists love. I name this part: *embody God's love.* This part of Walker's definition mentions how a womanist loves dancing and music, the moon and the Spirit. . . . "*Regardless.*" An important piece of this third part is a womanist loving their very being and culture, including the many ways in which they express that culture, such as dancing and music, and having that seen as valuable, sacred, and divine. Dancing and being musical are forms of play, along with spades, double Dutch, and hand games. Here Walker is stating that part of being a womanist is to have love for the body and love for play like the way God loves us: unconditionally.

The fourth part of Walker's definition is what Floyd-Thomas calls "critical engagement,"[5] which focuses on engaging justice and provides insight into the relationship of womanist to feminist, which has a similar relationship that purple has to lavender. I name this part: *enkindle the world,* as this deeper shade of purple is not necessarily at odds with lavender, but it demands a deeper and more passionate understanding and action for God's justice and equity in the world. While womanism lifts up the experience of Black women this does not negate the experiences of others; they can and should

3. Floyd-Thomas, *Mining the Motherlode*, 9.
4. Floyd-Thomas, *Mining the Motherlode*, 9–10.
5. Floyd-Thomas, *Mining the Motherlode*, 10–11.

coexist. However, womanism seeks to amplify the sacred experience of Black women, in order to expand our universal experience and understanding. It is this definition that provides the foundation for womanist theology, womanist ethics, womanist theological anthropology, and a womanist pedagogy of play.

Womanist Theology

"Womanist theology is critical reflection upon black women's place in the world that God has created and takes seriously black women's experience as human beings who are made in the image of God."[6] Given the history and reality of Black women, it is important to remember that Black women are not an accident or a mistake but were created in God's very image and likeness (Gen. 1:26). This means that Black women are not the stereotypes or roles forced upon us by the fantastic hegemonic imagination or the dominant group in power. This means that Black women are not the oversexualized and objectified entities that we are often made out to be. This means that Black women are not bitches or property but beautiful and beloved creations of God.

Womanist theology developed from Black women theologians and ethicists taking a closer look at Walker's work. Walker's description became a springboard for womanist pioneers into womanism and they created subsequent waves of womanism in various fields that continue to travel among other rising womanists. The beginning waves were created by trailblazing womanist scholars: Katie G. Cannon, Jacquelyn Grant, and Delores Williams. These three women all created critical awakenings through their scholarship and theological discourse such as Katie G. Cannon's *Black Womanist Ethics*, Jacquelyn Grant's *White Women's Christ and Black Women's Jesus*, and Delores Williams's *Sisters in the Wilderness*. All these womanist scholars take on the definition of womanism and what it means for the academy and our society at large. Theologian Delores Williams states:

6. Linda E. Thomas, "Womanist Theology, Epistemology, and a New Anthropological Paradigm," *Cross Currents* 48, no. 4 (Summer 1998): 488-99.

Womanist theology emerged from what many of us saw as characteristic of black women's experiences of relation, loss, gain, faith,
hope, celebration and defiance . . . womanist theology attempts to
help black women see, affirm and have confidence in the importance of their experience and faith for determining the character
of the Christian religion in the African-American community.
Womanist theology challenges all oppressive forces impeding
black women's struggle for survival and for the development of a
positive, productive quality of life conducive to women's and the
family's freedom and well-being. Womanist theology opposes all
oppression based on race, sex, class, sexual preference, physical
disability and caste.[7]

Williams states that womanism and womanist theology actively
resists oppression in all forms that might hinder one's freedom and
flourishing. She also notes that womanist theology gives Black women
an arena in and through which to share their stories, experiences, and
culture and to have those stories and experiences affirmed and lifted up
as important. I propose that part of the story, experience, and culture
of Black women are womanish modes of play that began in childhood
and continued into adulthood. Womanish modes of play connote the
various forms, ways, mediums, and types of play particular to, but
not exclusive to, the life and experience of Black girls and women.
These modes of play include playing games (like double Dutch and
spades), dancing, cooking, singing, conversing at the kitchen table,
painting, and many others. Many Black girls and women do not see
play as frivolous or irresponsible, but as a way of communicating,
making meaning, enacting agency, making decisions, forming moral
and ethical standards, expressing self, experiencing joy and rage, and
a way of finding a place of healing, renewal, and rejuvenation. Most
importantly we revel in play's function as liberative.

The reason we may or may not know about the playful side of
Black women is two-fold. For some it is because our play is sacred and

7. Delores Williams, *Sisters in the Wilderness: The Challenge of Womanist God-
Talk* (Maryknoll, NY: Orbis Books, 1993), xiv.

we don't desire to share that sacred part of who we are with colleagues and acquaintances, but only with those in our lives who care for, affirm, support, and truly see us. Another reason is that some Black women scholars feel the need to hide or diminish their play in order to be taken seriously and to be seen as significant in the academy and to be seen as "serious scholars." This is an example of Black women attempting to jump the one tightrope that has been made so very difficult to jump. Many Black women played as girls and that play has continued well into their lives as adults, but they are unable to openly express this play in their professional lives because of the stigma that playing is juvenile, unimportant, and pointless. Due to the race, gender, and class oppression that Black women experience in our society, often the need to be taken seriously supersedes the need to share or highlight one's playful embodied cultural expressions.

However, it is play that can operate as a source of renewal, be life-giving, offer hope and joy along with lament and rage amid racism and sexism within the academy. Womanish modes of play are ways in which Black women communicate, seek, and negotiate meaning in the world, specifically in the areas of ethical/moral, cognitive, and affective development. Play operates as a means of exploring identity as a Black girl becoming a Black woman who is made in the image of God. Play offers Black girls and Black women the freedom and courage to explore what it means to be both Black and woman. Growing, becoming, and changing are not easy, and play allows the space for the necessary fun and grace before, during, and after this transitional time.

Womanist Ethics

Womanist theology strives to take the fabrics of life and faith and to holistically weave them together.[8] As lives are intricate and filled with ethical and moral dilemmas, one cannot have or define a womanist

---

8. Stephanie Y. Mitchem, *Introducing Womanist Theology* (Maryknoll, NY: Orbis Books, 2002), xi.

theology without also explaining womanist ethics and moral formation. As theologian Stephanie Mitchem rightly asserts, "womanist theology must be grounded by womanist ethics. Such grounding is based on the complexities of lived experiences."[9] When the lived experiences of persons and communities are involved there must be an ethical and moral foundation provided.

Womanist ethics "seeks to determine how to eradicate oppressive social structures that limit and circumscribe the agency of African American women."[10] Based on Alice Walker's definition of womanism and the works of the womanist trailblazers, scholar, activist, and ethicist Stacey Floyd-Thomas lays out the four tenets of womanist ethics. In her book *Mining the Motherlode* Floyd-Thomas describes radical subjectivity, traditional communalism, redemptive self-love, and critical engagement as the four tenets of womanist ethics.

She names part one of Walker's definition of womanists being serious, responsible, audacious, and in charge as "radical subjectivity" (Floyd-Thomas, 8). Radical subjectivity is a womanist's "ability to grasp the radically subjective dimension of the 'nature vs. nurture' dialectic inherent within black women's moral formation" (Floyd-Thomas, 8). The dimension she mentions is among Black women who nurture and mentor young Black girls on how to navigate in a world where they must deal with racism, classism, and sexism—a triple jeopardy. This mentoring and maturing allows each woman involved to "claim her agency and have a subjective view of the world in which she is not a victim of circumstance, but rather is a responsible, serious, and in-charge woman" (Floyd-Thomas, 8). Radical subjectivism is being aware of systems of oppression and choosing to enact one's agency by resisting that dominant cultural system. This pushing back can happen through advocacy, legislation, protest, education for other Black women about these oppressive systems, and mentorship for them through the process by showing them the

9. Mitchem, *Introducing Womanist Theology*, 58.

10. Stacey M. Floyd-Thomas, *Mining the Motherlode: Methods in Womanist Ethics* (Cleveland: Pilgrim, 2006), 7. Hereafter, references to this source will appear in the text.

tightrope and how they might best jump it with the least amount of hurt and harm.

In the various types of womanish modes of play Black girls are introduced to the notion of nature vs. nurture[11] through mediums such as playing house. Through games such as playing house, Black women and girls learn how their gender and their color often affect what roles others think they should be playing in the world. When a young Black girl is encouraged by her playmates to be the nanny while playing house, this affects how she views herself as a Black girl. When a young Black girl is encouraged by her older Black sister to be a businesswoman, this too affects how she views herself as a Black girl, growing into a Black woman. During these moments of play, Black women and girls are afforded the agency to be aware of what is happening and to decide for themselves what roles they will and will not play as they become in-charge women. What Floyd-Thomas names as radical subjectivity I call *embracing self*.

The second part of Walker's definition concentrates on the wholeness of all people, which Floyd-Thomas names as "traditional communalism" (9) and I refer to as *engaging in culture and community*. Traditional communalism focuses on not just caring or writing about one's own desires and concerns, but about the life of one's entire community as a whole. In this area, womanist's work "encompasses not only the personal story of individual women; it also takes into account the various gifts, identities, and concerns of black people in general in order to use every resource available to strengthen the community as a whole" (9). Within womanism, it is the beloved Black community along with culture and history that keep womanist scholars supported and hold them accountable at the same time. For, this community often supports, prays for, uplifts, and sends care

11. A societal argument that looks at a person's behavior as either a developmental predisposition based on one's DNA (nature) or due to life experiences and environment (nurture). For example, there is an argument that women behave in a more caring and loving manner because they are biologically women not because they were raised in a particular environment. Womanists, however, would believe the latter, that one's experiences and environment influence their behavior.

packages to Black women while in school, in the military, or just figuring out life. And once she becomes an educator, doctor, actress, or beautician she gives back to the community that supported, mentored, and nurtured her. The Black woman knows that she does not do her work in a vacuum, but with, for, and to her community.

During play, Black women and girls are introduced to this notion of community. Just imagine a neighborhood game of tag. As folks gather from the neighborhood, there are different hues and genders that engage in play together. If someone falls, they are helped up to continue playing. If someone comes late, there is always space for them to join in. Through this mode of play, Black women and girls learn the importance of inclusion and the necessity to work together for the fun and survival of everyone. From play, Black women learn traditional communalism and promote the success of everyone, regardless of their gender, class, sexuality, ability, or color.

"Redemptive self-love" forms the third part of Walker's definition, which concentrates on what womanists love (9). Floyd-Thomas's third tenet of redemptive self-love explicates Walker's third notion in terms of "demystifying the perceptions of black women's bodies, ways, and love as vile" (9). Floyd-Thomas lifts up the idea of redeeming Black women's love for themselves and others. I refer to this redemptive self-love as *embodying God's love*. Given the historical realities and life experiences of Black women, this tenet holds particular importance. Being an enslaved surrogate sexual object does not cultivate a wealth of self-love, body-love, or self-worth. This tenet reminds Black women of their worth and their dignity as beings created in the image and likeness of God. This tenet does not stereotype the body as dangerous, criminal, or an object for sexual or pornographic misuse; rather the Black body was intentionally created by God as good, beautiful, powerful, life-giving, and worthy of rest and pleasure. This emphasis on the goodness and beauty of the body is a necessity for a group with a history of bodily oppression and abuse.

It is also important to accentuate the role that play has in this self-love and self-worth. Play provides space for agency and enacting self-love and self-worth through embodied expressions that can engender renewal and rejuvenation. So often Black women's bodies are seen as vile or over sexualized, which may affect their own self-worth and love. However, in playing, Black girls and women learn and are reminded how to love themselves and see themselves as absolutely beautiful and powerful. Just imagine playing dress-up, beauty shop, or making time for oneself. These are forms of play that allow Black women to be reminded of their beautiful and life-giving blackness. For example, doing a dance challenge or just putting on music and moving our bodies is powerful and liberating. Play is a reminder that Black women's bodies are important, have value, and deserve to take up space. In a society that values certain body types and skin colors over others, there is a need to be reminded of the beauty and strength of the Black woman's . . . everything!

Floyd-Thomas concludes with the fourth womanist tenet, "critical engagement" (10), which I refer to as *enkindle the world*. Floyd-Thomas mentions how womanism calls Black women to "critically engage their world at the intersection of their oppression." Black women work tirelessly for "freedom, justice, and equality" through critical engagement (11). Play offers the space to engage the world critically. When playing courthouse, debate, lawyer, president, or trivia, one must think critically about the problems of the world such as freedom, justice, and equality. These types of role-play and improvisation allow space for Black women and girls to think about critical issues that they might not normally think about and to engage these issues in new and significant ways from the perspective of a Black woman. These kinds of play prepare Black girls and women in a lower stakes environment to fight for what is fair and just. This preparation gives them confidence so that when the stakes are much higher, they continue to push back against all systems of oppression to fight for freedom and justice for all persons.

These tenets are areas in which women identifying as womanist find themselves engaging in and wrestling with their implementation. While these are not the only areas of engagement, they are the four that have been clearly spelled out by Floyd-Thomas. Play functions as one way in which Black women and girls can make meaning of their moral and ethical formation in the world. Play offers Black women and girls the freedom to explore the areas of radical subjectivity, traditional communalism, redemptive self-love, and critical engagement. Womanish modes of play such as playing house or a game of tag, doing makeovers, dancing, and debating are only a few of the modes of play in which Black women and girls can engage to explore these tenets, both in their lives and in the world. Play allows space for Black women to see their world anew (radical subjectivity/embrace self), to learn and appreciate the community from which they come (traditional communalism/engage in culture and community), to love themselves no matter what (redemptive self-love/embody God's love), and to be engaged as equals with freedom in the world around them (critical engagement/enkindle the world).

Womanist Theological Anthropology

Theology professors Cheryl Kirk-Duggan and Andrea White together offer a definition of a womanist theological anthropology as follows:

> Womanist theological anthropology involves an in-depth study of humanity amid the interconnectedness of biological, linguistic, and sociocultural systems as black women experience holistic life aware of oppressive systems of classism, racism, sexism, heterosexism, and ageism.[12]

Womanist theological anthropology reflects on how moral agency is negotiated and identity constructed when autonomy and self-definition cannot be taken for granted; how human agency, relationships and actions are read theologically; and what it means to

---

12. Cheryl A. Kirk-Duggan, "Signifying Love and Embodied Relationality: Toward a Womanist Theological Anthropology," in *Womanist and Black Feminist Responses to Tyler Perry's Productions*, ed. LeRhonda S. Manigault-Bryant, Tamura A. Lomax, and Carol B. Duncan (New York: Palgrave Macmillan, 2014), 43.

say that identity and the *imago Dei* are understood as theological and ethical tasks.[13]

Black women not only understand the notion of double consciousness, but they live it every single day. Black women are continually aware of the contradiction of the oppressive systems that are indeed part of our daily lived experience. Black women's desire and need for survival and liberation through Jesus Christ arise from the constant oppressive reality of being both Black and a woman in this world.

During times of oppression, both current and in the past, Black women found hope in Jesus knowing that he suffers with us and yet rises with the hope of new life for us all. Womanist theological anthropology takes a critical look at this reality and assesses all oppressive systems along with their personal and communal values. Womanist theological anthropology views personal and communal values as one, since relationships and community engender agency, change, transformation, and flourishing.[14] One is not separate from the community in which they are formed, supported, and challenged. They are also not only striving for their own liberation but for the liberation of their community and for all of God's children.[15]

Womanist theological anthropology understands and highlights the multiplicity of one's identity and formation in this world. Intersectional identity and being is key for womanist theological anthropology,[16] which welcomes the various intersections in ways of knowing, being, and embodied expression. This includes mediums such as

---

13. Andrea C. White, course description for her "Theological Anthropology in Womanist Thought" class at Union Theological Seminary, Fall 2016.

14. Kirk-Duggan, "Signifying Love and Embodied Relationality," 43.

15. Kirk-Duggan, "Signifying Love and Embodied Relationality," 43.

16. This is the cross-pollination of categories such as race, class, gender, and sexuality. The overlapping of these categories often creates even more disadvantage and discrimination than what might be had with identifying with just one of these categories. This is what is meant with the metaphor of purple to lavender when thinking about womanism and feminism. While feminism looks at gender, womanism looks at the interconnectedness of gender, race, and class in regard to Black women.

music, food, poetry, dance, and play. These creative means engender vulnerability while valuing differences that can be salvific and liberating.[17] Womanist theological anthropology values the entirety of a person in body, mind, and spirit. Striving for justice, liberation, and empowerment, womanist theological anthropology celebrates all persons, especially the marginalized, as created in the image and likeness of God, and having worth, dignity, and freedom.[18]

> Womanist theology is the positive affirmation of the gifts, which God has given black women in the U. S. A. It is, within theological discourse, an emergent voice which advocates a holistic God-talk for all the oppressed. Though centered in the African American woman's reality and story, it also embraces and stands in solidarity with all suppressed subjects. In a word, womanist theology is a theory and practice of inclusivity, accenting gender, race, class, sexual orientation, and ecology. Because of its inclusive methodology and conceptual framework, womanist theology exemplifies reconstructed knowledge beyond the monovocal concerns of black (male) and (white) feminist theologies.[19]

Womanist theologian Linda Thomas argues that by attending carefully to the lives and experiences of Black women, we can see God-given gifts amid the injustices of racial and sexist oppression. This womanist rope brings awareness to broken systems while actively advocating for agency, change, and an inclusive solidarity that will bring freedom for all those who are suppressed and disinherited. Womanist thinking, knowing, and being does not only see Black women but a community of marginalized persons of various colors, sexual and gender identities, and abilities that deserve freedom and justice as creations of a just God.[20] This type of theology, ethics, and

---

17. Kirk-Duggan, "Signifying Love and Embodied Relationality," 52.
18. Kirk-Duggan, "Signifying Love and Embodied Relationality," 54-55.
19. Thomas, "Womanist Theology, Epistemology, and a New Anthropological Paradigm," *Cross Currents* 48, no. 4 (Summer 1998): 488-99.
20. Thomas, "Womanist Theology," 43.

theological anthropology allows us all to view others and ourselves in a more holistic way as beings with multiple identities made in the image of God. It is not just the mind that is made in God's image and likeness, but it is also the heart, body, and entirety of a person.

Womanism hears and sees those who have gone unheard and unseen.

Womanism honors the stories of those who have been overlooked and forgotten.

Womanism advocates for a radical inclusivity of communities to resist injustice and to fight oppressive systems for the freedom of all of God's people.

Chapter 6

Does Mother Play?

I define play as *an embodied aesthetic experience and a cultural expression that are a part of what it means to be human. This play functions as a way of knowing, being, and making meaning in the world.* This definition denotes play as an inclusive experience that provides a distinctly womanist conception of cultural expression that both advances and departs from prevailing notions of play that will be discussed more in depth in part 3. Given womanists' commitment to inclusion, cultural histories and realities, intersectionality of knowing, being, and embodiment, I sought to offer a definition of play that was equally inclusive and aware of cultural histories and realities.

Some Black women have had to become critically aware in order to survive in the world in an attempt to challenge the dominant racist and sexist narrative and social formation. Play as a part of human nature functions as a means of creating one's own meaning, allowing its players to be and become radically aware and to practice and eventually enact ways in which to challenge the dominant narrative.

Womanists believe in the power of their community and the necessity of everyone making it together. We believe in helping each other, being accountable for one another, and standing in solidarity, together, against injustices. This belief allows for the pooling of resources to help the greater community at large. As a cultural expression, play engenders this kind of community and allows for remembering one's own culture and community, while at the same time engaging and coming to know and understand another's culture and community.

Some Black women have had the narrative of being worthless, sexual objects forced upon them. Self-worth and self-love are not just desires for Black women, but *necessities* not simply to survive but to *thrive* in the world. Play as an embodied aesthetic experience allows space for ownership and appreciation of one's body, beauty, dignity, and cultivates one's faith in God as one sees oneself as made in the image of God. It allows space for one to get to know oneself and one's body, and to come to truly see and know who one is. Play can engender self-worth, dignity, and love.

Many Black women were raised to not engage the world for fear of being misunderstood, or being treated as having a lack of intelligence, or even facing the threat of violent death. Play provides a space to wrestle with what is happening with the world and oneself considering one's own beliefs and ideas, hopes, and dreams. Play can operate as a space for negotiating meaning and trying things out. This experience can create a critical engagement with things happening in the world and bring to the surface many feelings and emotions that were previously under the surface—and thus were unknown. The experience of play can build confidence and agency that leads to enacting change toward justice for all. In this sense play functions as an act of liberation in which persons can embrace part of their human nature, express their cultural histories and realities, and experience themselves and God in their bodies and the world. This inclusive and distinctly womanist kind of play is an experience and expression by which all persons can be formed and informed, and through a ready medium that can lead to change and transformation.

Culture and cultural expression are key aspects in womanist theory and practice, womanist theology, ethics, and theological anthropology; moreover, culture and cultural expression are pertinent and unique to my definition of play. Therefore, it is important to clarify what is meant by culture and cultural expression in this work. "Culture" refers to that community and ethos into which one was born, within which one is raised and lives, by which one is formed in identity and meaning making, and which serves as the principal context from which one relates to the world. For each of these stages of life there might be a different culture and community and they are each important and impactful. There are many intersectional layers to one's cultural reality that include gender, religion, race, class, social location, nationality, geographic location, ethnicity, orientation, ability, and many others. Culture is not just one stagnant thing, but the fluidity and convergence of many influences and sources.

Different cultures play differently as a matter of their own historical realities, resources, and learned behavior as a cultural group. Cultures have often evolved through various forms of play, which explains why it is important to know that play can also be culturally particular.[1] Play functions as a way in which people express core and religious morals, values, and truths and is affected by one's cultural history and experience.

People's play is a reflection and expression of their culture and identity-community—whether they want it to be or not. For example, playing house could look different for persons from different cultural groups. Many Black girls may have grown up getting their hair straightened with a hot comb.[2] During this process there was often laughter, tears, burning, and conversation. A woman from India might not share this experience; therefore, when the young Black girl attempts to straighten the Indian girl's hair with an imaginary hot comb while playing house, she might have to explain exactly what she is doing. In this way they are both learning about themselves and another culture through the play. It is through this inclusive play that we can learn and begin to appreciate and understand our own culture and the culture of others. Play invites others into the community as each player expresses themselves and their culture and each player learns how to negotiate, communicate, and make meaning with other players.

It is with diversity in mind that a conversation with theologian Kathryn Tanner becomes helpful. In her work, Tanner contrasts a

1. Johan Huizinga, *Homo Ludens: A Study of the Play Element in Culture* (Boston: Beacon, 1950), foreword.
2. The hot comb is a heavy metal comb that is warmed on the stove. The hot metal is then combed through the hair in order to straighten it.

modern and postmodern understanding of culture and advocates for the latter, as applied within theology and anthropology. First, she lists nine basic elements of a modern meaning. For Tanner, modern culture: (1) is a human universal, (2) highlights human diversity, (3) varies with social group, (4) is seen as an entire way of life, (5) is associated with social consensus, (6) constructs human nature, (7) is a human construction, (8) is contingent to its context, (9) and advances social determinism.[3] She then dissects this into six parts to describe a more postmodern and porous understanding of culture.

In her postmodern shift of culture, Tanner recognizes, first, the inattention to history and the historical struggle (40-42). This is particularly important for this work, given the historical reality of Black women in the United States. Second, this reconstructed culture is against viewing cultures as wholes, since bits and pieces of culture become present at any time, given that particular situation, circumstance, and people involved (42-45). Third, this postmodern culture is also against consensus as it doesn't give voice to conflict and the ways in which "different senses are given to cultural elements" (45-47). Fourth, postmodern culture is against culture as a principle of social order, which can often idealize a culture into one set of beliefs and values. Every member of a culture may or may not genuinely hold a certain value or belief. While values and beliefs of a particular culture often shape the actions that follow, one would be remiss to attribute that solely to a social order and not think of various historical realities that might affect each person differently (47-51). "What is reactionary in one context may be subversive in another" (49).

A fifth aspect of this reconstruction of culture is being against cultural stability. Culture itself has "principles of change" that are fluid and loosely connected allowing them to be "ordered and reordered" throughout time and circumstance (51-53). Lastly, this reconstructed postmodern culture is against cultures as self-contained units with sharp boundaries. The postmodern idea of culture without sharp

---

3. Kathryn Tanner, *Theories of Culture: A New Agenda for Theology* (Minneapolis: Fortress, 1997), 26-29. Hereafter, references to this source will appear in the text.

boundaries makes space for conflict and change, which no longer allows the political and historical realities of inequality to remain unaddressed (53–56).

This postmodern reconstruction of cultural expression considers historical reality by not viewing cultures as a whole social order with consensus, stability, and sharp boundaries, but one that is fluid and ebbs and flows through conflict and change as life happens. This notion of cultural expression acknowledges differences among and within cultures and the need for ordering and reordering in light of circumstances and the realization of inequality—wherever they occur. It is this notion of cultural expression that makes a space for an inclusive and welcoming womanist understanding of play.

To understand play as a cultural expression suggests that in play one acknowledges the historical realities of groups, spaces, and places in which persons were born, raised, and currently live. This includes those communities and cultures that were both chosen and not chosen. It also recognizes that groups borrow and repurpose their own cultural elements, tools, rules, etc. rather than inventing them solely for the purpose of the game. The fluidity that exists makes play more relevant to "real life," since one must learn to change and adapt to any given situation. Play allows one to order and then reorder as life experiences, cultural realities, and world circumstances see fit. Play isn't a fringe, irrelevant thing but a core piece of who one is in the world and operates in a way that allows one to make meaning within that world. Therefore, whether one wants it to or not, play is and will always be a cultural expression that acknowledges the many cultural histories and realities into which one is born, raised, and currently lives.

Chapter 7

Does Mother's Body Matter?

In understanding womanism and the importance of the bodymind in play, one must discuss the body. The experience of Black women's bodies is colored by the history of slavery in the United States. The Black woman's body has been pillaged and seen as evil, often being viewed as chattel and a commodity as described in part 1. Even today the bodies of Black women continue to be coerced, abused, and hyper-sexualized.[1] Many Black women experience racism, sexism, ageism, ableism, homophobia, transphobia, and other types of oppression against their bodies and personhood. As theologian Cheryl Townsend Gilkes states, "For African-American women, the pain of simply being embodied—coping with others' responses to our hair, skin, and size— can overshadow the strengths and options. The pathetic dimension too often obscures the heroic possibilities."[2] The very being of Black women brings unsolicited responses, attacks, and degradation. Being Black is an obstacle by itself in the academy. Being a woman is an obstacle by itself in the academy. By merely being a Black woman, one already begins jumping this tightrope with two huge obstacles. These realities are reasons why the rope of womanism is needed to be critical of and challenge these oppressive and unjust systems.

Womanism, womanist theology, womanist ethics, and womanist theological anthropology affirm the beauty of Black women, Black

---

1. Kelly Brown Douglas, *Stand Your Ground: Black Bodies and the Justice of God* (Maryknoll, NY: Orbis Books, 2005), 65.

2. Cheryl Townsend Gilkes, *If It Wasn't for the Women* (Maryknoll, NY: Orbis Books, 2001), 188.

women's experiences, Black women's bodies, and also affirm Black women as made in the image and likeness of God, and therefore holding dignity and honor. They affirm a particular marginalized group, and by doing so highlight the personhood of all people by bringing awareness, recognition, and dismantling of systems of oppression that exist within the interconnectedness of the lives of people.

The history of the enslavement of Black women is a reality. The need to resist the fantastic hegemonic imagination that runs rampant in our country is also a reality. Play as a cultural expression provides the space to actively resist and becomes a medium for meaning making, identity formation, and rejuvenation. In addition, play uniquely offers a physical, bodily release to persons who have been marginalized, oppressed, and subjugated. Theologian Phillis Isabella Sheppard states that "our [black women] bodies, rather than experienced as good, pleasurable, and integral to who we are—to ourselves but also to each other—have become the scapegoats for internalized black body ambivalence."[3] This Black body ambivalence has come as a result of years of enslavement, abuse, objectification, and coercion. These bodies that have taken so much and need a release that play can offer. These bodies that have encountered experiences of abuse, pain, and suffering need to be free; play allows an avenue for that freedom. This play can operate in a way that gives people freedom to be who they are and to experience themselves, for themselves. This kind of ontological space to be oneself and to come to know for oneself is necessary for reclaiming one's bruised and hurt body, for self-love, for body-love, for self-worth and for encountering God in our bodiliness.

As beings created in God's image, Black women, and all people for that matter, are called by God to make moral decisions to fight and struggle for the justice of God which is "a restoration of the sacred dignity of all people."[4] All bodies are sacred and holy as they are created in the *imago Dei* and this includes the bodies of Black women.

---

3. Phillis Isabella Sheppard, *Self, Culture, and Others in Womanist Practical Theology* (New York: Palgrave Macmillan, 2011), 48.

4. Douglas, *Stand Your Ground*, 197.

The bodies of Black women can become sites of resistance against oppression and injustice, especially in this North American context that still experiences the legacy of racism and slavery so deeply. Play is one space where Black women can begin to create ontological/free space.[5] This resistance has renewed urgency in the United States today.

In the Flesh

Slavery stripped away the joy of embodied aesthetic experience and movement as well as the dignity, honor, and bodies of many people, including Black women. Theologian M. Shawn Copeland speaks of this passionately: "Slavery rendered black women's bodies objects of property, of production, of reproduction, of sexual violence." In the centuries since then, "black female bodies have continually been defiled, used, and discarded, quite literally, as refuse—simply because they are female and black, black and female."[6] Just turn on the television to view how Hollywood portrays Black women as mistresses, sluts, bitches, amazing professionals with their personal lives in tatters, and harlots incapable of healthy sexual and familial relationships. I mention the stereotyping and caricatures of Black women in part 1 as mouthy, overly complicated, suspicious, dysfunctional, and as sexual or bodily objects of desire, pleasure, and entertainment. Black women are still viewed as incomplete and segmented beings with a brilliant mind here, an impressive vertical jump there, great eyes, and big hair. But rarely are Black women seen as complete persons. Because they are Black and woman, Black women are dismembered, exploited, and often not viewed as whole human beings.

However, one can begin to address systematic oppression by not only looking at the body "in the flesh" but by also looking at what happens to the flesh of the body as well. This begins by first looking

5. M. Shawn Copeland, *Enfleshing Freedom: Body, Race, and Being* (Minneapolis: Fortress, 2010), 18, 153.
6. Copeland, *Enfleshing Freedom*, 1, 29.

at the incarnation of God in Jesus. This is the "enfleshment"[7] of God in Jesus Christ, who was both divine and human. Womanist ethicist Eboni Marshall Turman explains that when one looks at the incarnation one must not only remember what "occurs *en sarki,* 'in the flesh,' but also what occurs *kata sarka,* or 'according to the flesh.'"[8] The incarnation is what happened *in* the flesh of Jesus Christ. God became flesh *in* the human body of Jesus Christ (John 1:14). Thereafter all human flesh is made holy, of God. This includes the flesh of the marginalized and oppressed bodies. For Black women the moving of the Holy Spirit is what is happening *in* the flesh of each person.

However, thankfully, the story of the body does not end there with the birthing but continues on to the dying and rising of Christ. The passion and resurrection are what happened *to* Jesus's body. His body was abused and beaten to death, just as many Black women's bodies were and continue to be beaten and abused. These are things that happened *to* the body. These happenings to the body were outward manifestations of oppression. It is only when what happens *in* the body and what happens *to* the body are held together that one can begin to understand the importance of the future coming or parousia of Christ and most importantly—hope.[9] We have hope "because we know that the one who raised Jesus will raise us also with Jesus, and will present us with you in his presence" (2 Cor. 4:14). The fact that God raised up Jesus's body gives hope now to all beaten bodies just as Jesus's rising also raises up all who have been beaten down to "walk in newness of life" (Rom. 6:4). It is in the realization that both what happens *in* and *to* the body matter. That the hope in the birthing, dying, and rising of Jesus—and the justice and freedom he stood for during his public life with his preaching of the kin-dom[10] of God are

---

7. See Eboni Marshall Turman, *Toward a Womanist Ethic of Incarnation: Black Bodies, the Black Church, and the Council of Chalcedon* (New York: Palgrave Macmillan, 2013), 49.

8. Turman, *Toward a Womanist Ethic of Incarnation*, 43. Emphasis added.

9. Turman, *Toward a Womanist Ethic of Incarnation*, 42.

10. I prefer to use this term *kin-dom* over *kingdom.* This phrase, an adaptation of the theological symbol of the "kingdom/reign of God," was coined by Cuban-American *mujerista* theologian Ada María Isasi-Díaz as a way of problematizing

needed for any attempt of justice, liberation, and transformation. Turman asserts that, "this innovative politics of incarnation, rather the deployment of incarnational logic recognizes the potentiality of black women's bodies as the image of the broken body of Christ in the world, and thus, black women as the very incarnation (enfleshment) of hope."[11] Here Turman draws a link between what happened to the broken body of Christ and the broken bodies of Black women. She uses incarnational logic to assert that the experiences that happen to the bodies of both Jesus and Black women allow the potential to see parallels in their bodily experiences and thus offer something more for life after being broken and beaten. The birthing, living, dying, and rising of Jesus offers hope. A hope that sustains through being beaten and bruised. A hope that endures through oppression, subjugation, and surrogacy. A hope that recognizes the beauty and necessity of the body along with the soul. A hope that challenges systems of oppression that would seek to dismember, beat, and abuse the body. A hope that lives in and through the bodies of Black women. A hope that gives life after.

Bodies as Playful Sites of Resistance

Some may not understand the incarnational logic of Turman nor see the value in the body, especially the bodies of Black women. Even today the bodies of Black women continue to be beaten, abused, and viewed as incomplete.[12] Now, there is an additional factor of Black women's bodies being seen as dangerous, guilty, and criminal,

---

the imperialism and dominance inherent in the traditional formulation. As an alternative, kin-dom highlights God's activity in and orientation toward familial care, inclusion, solidarity, and unity. See Ada María Isasi-Díaz, "Kin-dom of God: A Mujerista Proposal," in In Our Own Voices: Latino/a Renditions of Theology, ed. Benjamín Valentín (Maryknoll, NY: Orbis Books, 2010), 171–90; Ada María Isasi-Díaz, Mujerista Theology: A Theology for the Twenty-First Century (Maryknoll, NY: Orbis Books, 1996).

11. Turman, Toward a Womanist Ethic of Incarnation, 49.

12. Douglas, Stand Your Ground, 65.

merely because of their brown and black hues.[13] Black women and Black women's bodies have a long history of not being their own and continue to be places of contention. These continued instances of oppression raise the question of God and where God is in these injustices: theodicy. Womanism, womanist theology, womanist ethics, and womanist theological anthropology affirm the beauty, experiences, and bodies of Black women. The bodies of Black women can become sites of resistance against oppression and injustice. Theologian M. Shawn Copeland offers five basic convictions that must ground this conversation about God and the body. She asserts, "The body is a site and mediation of divine revelation; that the body shapes human existence as relational and social; that the creativity of the Triune God is manifested in differences of gender, race, and sexuality; that solidarity is a set of body practices; and that the Eucharist orders and transforms our bodies as the body of Christ."[14] This connection with Christ and the Black body are united because, in using the incarnational logic of Turman, "in his suffering and crucifixion, Jesus embraces and proleptically unites the real suffering of black bodies to his own."[15] In solidarity and love with the other, one becomes re-made. In this remaking "we are all transformed in Christ: we are his very own flesh." In thinking about the Black body in this way we begin to view the Black body as a "site of divine revelation."[16] The body becomes a medium for doing the work of God, including combating oppression and fighting for the justice of God and the liberation of all people.

If we truly adhere to both White's and Kirk-Duggan's notions of a theological anthropology that is distinctly womanist, then one must believe that each person was uniquely created by God. This means one must honor and respect each person's difference to bring about an inclusivity that does more than tolerate or overcome but truly respects and welcomes difference. One must come to a place of unity where everyone is responsible for living out their faith by being moral

13. Douglas, *Stand Your Ground*, 68, 48, 77.
14. Copeland, *Enfleshing Freedom*, 2.
15. Copeland, *Enfleshing Freedom*, 5.
16. Copeland, *Enfleshing Freedom*, 83, 82, 24.

73

agents of change and correcting injustices.[17] This involves not only considering what is happening *in* the body but also what happens *to* the body.

The body is sacred and holy as it is uniquely created in the *imago Dei*. It is with this body that one can begin to create ontological[18] or free space[19] and make one's body a site of resistance to the oppression and injustices in the world. One can proclaim, as poet Letitia Hodge does:

> I'm a woman of purpose and destiny.
>
> A perfect design, I'm special and unique.
> I won't be identified by the parts that make up my physique.[20]

It is with the body that Black women can see the dignity, beauty, and humanity in their own bodies and use that agency in their fight for liberation, body autonomy, and the justice of God in the world for all bodies.

American activist and filmmaker Brittany "Bree" Newsome from Charlotte, North Carolina, is a prime example of how the body can be a source of social justice for womanist liberation. In the midst of national unrest around the history, nature, racist culture, and symbolism of the confederate flag, on June 27, 2015, Brittany made a decision to stand against this injustice. She went to the South Carolina Statehouse grounds, climbed up the flagpole and removed the confederate flag. Brittany used her body as a site of resistance against the racist nature and history that the confederate flag symbolized by removing it from a place of power. She was arrested for this act, and in doing so she stirred more unrest and put pressure on state officials.

17. Marcia Y. Riggs, *Awake, Arise, and Act: A Womanist Call for Black Liberation* (Cleveland: Pilgrim, 1994), 93–97.

18. Copeland, *Enfleshing Freedom*, 18.

19. Douglas, *Stand Your Ground*, 153.

20. Letitia Hodge, *My Pledge of Allegiance to Me*, 2004, http://www.tribute toblackwomen.com/poems/pledge.htm.

This act resulted in the confederate flag being permanently removed from the South Carolina Statehouse, as of July 10, 2015. Brittany's body and actions fought for social justice and liberation, and won.

Play is not the answer to all the problems Black women face, but it can aid them in taking back their Black bodies from society's claim of ownership. Black women can embrace their bodies as their own, and more significantly, as bodies uniquely created in the *imago Dei*, that is, in the image of a free, creative, and wonderful Creator. Through play, Black women can begin to see their bodies not only as sites of theological reflection, but resistance as well. This requires the internalization of the words of M. Shawn Copeland, who writes, "The body is the medium through which the person as essential freedom achieves and realizes selfhood through communion with other embodied selves." Through play as an embodied aesthetic experience and cultural expression one is better able to embrace their beautiful blackness and to encourage others to embrace themselves. As Copeland states so powerfully, "To declare 'black is beautiful!' states a disregarded theological truth, nourishes and restores bruised interiority, prompts memory, encourages discovery and recovery, stimulates creativity and acknowledges and reverences the wholly Other. To assert, 'beauty is black' exorcises the 'ontological curse' that consigns the black body to the execrable, and claims ontological space: space to be, space to realize one's humanity authentically. I am black and beautiful."[21]

The assertion of one's beauty and body requires space. This space must be one in which historical realities are known and individuals are free to be themselves and to explore their identities apart from the ones that were placed on them by the dominant group. The theological classroom can begin to provide this clearing space that allows for the celebration of all identities, while still recognizing and holding accountable systems of oppression that would prevent certain persons from embracing and expressing their bodily identities.

This embodiment needs an outlet that happens during play. It is important to remember that play takes on many forms. Play can be

21. Copeland, *Enfleshing Freedom*, 18.

cooking, dancing, painting, coloring, and even resting. In her book, *Rest Is Resistance*, Tricia Hersey states, "Our bodies are a site of liberation. We are divine and our rest is divine. Rest is a healing portal to our deepest selves. Rest is care. Rest is radical . . . rest is a form of resistance because it disrupts and pushes back against capitalism and white supremacy. Both these toxic systems refuse to see the inherent divinity in human beings and have used bodies as a tool for production, evil, and destruction for centuries."[22] This kind of rest and embodiment allows for reflection not just of what is happening *in* the body but also what is happening *to* the body. Reflection and meditation bring awareness of the systems of oppression and engender a desire to respect difference, strive for an authentic unity, and hold each other responsible for living out faith by combating injustices when and wherever they arise. One way of combating injustices is by making the body a site of resistance. One means of engaging the body as a site of resistance is through various modes of play that are embodied aesthetic experiences and cultural expressions, like resting, climbing a flagpole, dancing, protesting, singing, and using the body in various ways to resist oppressive systems and fight for the liberation of all people.

22. Tricia Hersey, *Rest Is Resistance: A Manifesto* (New York: Little, Brown Spark, 2022), vi.

Chapter 8

Womanish Modes of Play

Engage in Culture and Community

Here is the second part of the womanist definition and the accompanying ethical tenet of womanism from Alice Walker and Stacey Floyd-Thomas.

A woman who loves other women, sexually and/or nonsexually. Appreciates and prefers women's culture, women's emotional flexibility (values tears as natural counterbalance of laughter) and women's strength. Sometimes loves individual men, sexually and/or nonsexually. Committed to survival and wholeness of entire people, male *and* female. Not a separatist, except periodically for health. Traditionally universalist, as in: "Mama, why are we brown, pink, and yellow, and our cousins are white, beige, and black?" Ans.: "Well, you know the colored race is just like a flower garden, with every color flower represented." Traditionally capable, as in: "Mama, I'm walking to Canada and I'm taking you and a bunch of other slaves with me." Reply: "It wouldn't be the first time."[1]

Womanist ethicists engage in scholarly compositions that hold them accountable not to their individual whims or personalized localized consciousness but rather to the collective values of black history and culture. In illustrating a spirit of traditional communalism, the work of womanist ethicists encompasses not only the

---

1. Walker, *In Search of Our Mothers' Gardens: Womanist Prose* (New York: Harcourt, Brace, 1983), xi–xii. Emphasis original.

personal story of individual women; it also takes into account the
various gifts, identities, and concerns of black people in general in
order to use every resource available to strengthen the community
as a whole.[2]

The focus here is on inclusivity and community. It reminds everyone that we are all intersectional persons with many gifts, experiences, and cultures that intertwine in our lives. Womanism sees
these differences and various experiences as a gift to be appreciated,
valued, amplified, and loved . . . regardless. All these experiences are
what make up the whole person and womanism is committed to the
survival and flourishing of all people, not just Black women. While
Black women come from a unique history and experience, it is that
experience of struggle and survival that pushes us to fight so hard for
the inclusion and wholeness of every single person regardless of race,
gender, ethnicity, religion, ability, political views, and/or sexual orientation. This commitment for wholeness and flourishing leads to a
level of accountability to one's community, history, and culture. This
means that no person gets left behind or forgotten, but that everyone
comes together. This means that people stay to help those coming
behind them. This means that networks of mentorship are developed
to help others. This means that everyone can win, when everyone is
committed to the thriving and flourishing of all people. It must start
with the knowledge that God desires liberation and flourishing for
everyone. This knowledge comes from connecting with God's liberating actions in the Christian narrative through biblical texts. Once one
has read and encountered various texts of God's liberating actions in
the world one can then know without a shadow of a doubt, regardless
of the dominant narrative, that God desires and has acted in ways for
all persons to be free.

This kind of commitment engenders a radical sense of inclusivity and community that can be difficult to cultivate, but even more
difficult to dismantle. To make the classroom a radically inclusive

2. Stacey M. Floyd-Thomas, *Mining the Motherlode: Methods in Womanist
Ethics* (Cleveland: Pilgrim, 2006), 9.

space, educators must cultivate ways to create this kind of radical culture within the classroom community. To help create this kind of environment and to aid participants in the process of becoming committed to this kind of radical inclusivity and classroom culture and community the educator can offer womanish modes of play that promote appreciative inclusion, communal accountability, and bonding. These womanish modes of play can be, but are not limited to cooking and eating together, playing card/board games, doing line dancing, and doing hand jives/games.

Essentials and Suggestions

Each of these womanish modes of play stems from a womanist consciousness, culture, and experience. The modes of play mentioned above—cooking and eating together, playing card/board games, doing line dancing, and doing hand jives/games—invite participants to get to know each other in new and different ways, which can lead to more appreciation of diversity and create classroom and group bonding. I have come to discover that violence, microaggressions, and macroaggressions in the classroom often stem from a fear of the unknown and difference. However, the kind of inclusive classroom that involves womanish modes of play can allow for teaching and learning across differences with both fewer microaggressions and acts of violence and more calling out when they do happen which leads to dialogue, as students begin to truly see and appreciate diversity instead of fear it.

In the Christian narrative there are many stories of liberation and of God's liberating acts. Taking time during these modes of play to connect to these stories is vital. Just think about how God liberated Israel from the hands of the Egyptians in the book of Exodus. God believes in and desires liberation of God's people from injustice. In order to resist and push for flourishing and freedom for all, as a Christian, one must know that "doing justice" (Mic. 6:8) and striving for flourishing and freedom are not only what God intended for us, but how we live out God's call, spread God's love, and live into God's wholeness.

Through these modes of play participants can begin to see and understand more about each other's history, heritage, and culture and hopefully gain more appreciation for all that each person brings to the classroom space. As participants begin to appreciate and value each other they begin to bond, care for each other, and hold each other accountable for holding space and sitting in creative tension that is welcoming, inclusive, challenging, and liberative.

Womanish Modes of Play: Engaging Culture and Community

- *Womanish mode of play:* Cooking and eating together.
- *Materials needed:* If just eating, students will need food and utensils to eat with such as plates and silverware. If cooking and eating, students will need both time and necessary food items or recipes in order to prepare the meal and then space and utensils to eat the meal.
- *Environment/space:* Space for cooking and preparation and space for eating together.
- *Directions:* After discussing the importance of engaging culture and community, invite your students to set aside time for cooking or eating together. Invite them to discuss and decide together what they will cook or order to eat with each other. Invite them to discuss and decide together who will cook or order, set the table, clean up, etc. Invite them to be fully present with one another, to deeply listen and share—to engage in culture and community together.
- *Questions for reflection:*
  - What was made/ordered and why?
  - What did you choose to eat and why?
  - How was the food prepared/ordered? Was a recipe used? Which one and why?
  - How do you feel about what you cooked/ordered and ate?
  - How did it taste?
  - What stories were shared?
  - What did you learn about your cooking and dining partner(s)?

- *Womanish mode of play:* Line dancing.
- *Materials needed:* Music to be played and a tool to play the music on (i.e., speakers, band, instrument, etc.).
- *Environment/space:* A dance floor or a large flat space for movement and dancing.
- *Directions:* After discussing the importance of engaging in culture and community, invite your students to do a line dance together. This also works well to do even before a discussion. Line dances are specific dances that are taught and done together. The dance is a series of moves that are repeated over and over until everyone is able to dance it together in unison. A few line dances that are widely known are the Electric Slide, the Cupid Shuffle, the Cha Cha Slide, and the Wobble. If your students know the dance, you can invite them to help someone who doesn't. If your students don't know it, you can invite them to jump in and learn by doing. Once the dance is learned, students are welcome to add their own personal style and flair. As with all play, if someone doesn't feel comfortable there is always the option to witness—not passively observe but to be an active witness who is engaged, fully present, and involved in engaging culture and community.
- *Questions for reflection:*
  - Did you know the line dance when you started? If not, did you know it by the end?
  - How did it feel to dance with other people?
  - What did you learn about yourself?
  - What did you learn about your dance partner(s)?
  - What is lingering with you?

- *Womanish mode of play:* Playing board game/card games.
- *Materials needed:* The necessary pieces of the particular board or card game.
- *Environment/space:* A place with a table to play on, chairs or space for players to sit, and space for people to laugh and joke in high volumes without disturbing others.
- *Directions:* After discussing the importance of engaging in culture and community, invite your students to play a game. Invite your

students to discuss and decide what game to play together. They should discuss and agree on the rules together, before the game begins as well. Then they should play and enjoy engaging in culture and community as the game unfolds.

- *Questions for reflection:*
  - What game did you play?
  - Have you played this game before? If so, how or why was it different this time?
  - Did you all know and practice the same rules?
  - What did you learn about yourself? About your play partner(s)?
  - What is lingering with you?

- *Womanish mode of play:* Doing hand jives/childhood games.
- *Materials needed:* Various pieces depending on the game (e.g., two jump ropes for double Dutch or chalk and a sidewalk for hopscotch).
- *Environment/space:* Open space for playing and loud voices.
- *Directions:* After discussing the importance of engaging culture and community, invite your students to do a hand jive or outdoor childhood game. Once they discuss and decide on a hand jive or a game to play together, they should discuss the rules before playing. Then they should play and enjoy engaging in culture and community as the play unfolds.
- *Questions for reflection:*
  - What game did you play?
  - Have you played this game before? If, so how or why was it different this time?
  - Did you all know and practice the same rules?
  - What did you learn about yourself?
  - What did you learn about your play partner(s)?
  - How did you feel after?
  - What is lingering with you?

Practical Example of Engaging Culture and Community

While teaching a class, I wanted to engage my students in dialogue around the different contexts and cultures they embodied. It was still toward the beginning of the semester, and I was not sure if participants were ready to address issues of race, identity, ethnicity, and sexuality in an honest and open way yet. So, I decided to surprise them one class. While they were walking into the classroom I started playing "The Cupid Shuffle." (Thankfully I already knew the dance so I could start it off!) The only instructions were: "Move as you feel led. There is no right or wrong." As I started moving, the students suspiciously began to jump in. One person after another joined in. Some sat out and participated as witnesses of those who were dancing. Some were learning the dance for the first time and others adding their own personal style, but all were laughing, teaching each other, and moving bodies *together*.

After we finished, I began to reflect on the many Scriptures that spoke of dance. I asked them to read and reflect on the power of dance in the Scripture and what it might have in common with our dance today. This led to a discussion about dancing in times of joy and lament and how dancing brings connection and relationship. These conversations continued as students noted how each of them brought their own style and uniqueness to the dance, and how that made the space and the dance better. Several students agreed and mentioned other students' styles. I then mentioned how each of them also brought their own God-given talents and unique styles and experiences into the classroom, which only enriched the space. I mentioned that regardless of their differences there was enough space for everyone's dance. I invited them to spend a few moments creatively and collaboratively imagining our class as the dance we just did. I invited them to think about what each of their different styles and cultures brings to the classroom space. One after another they began to dialogue about what they experienced from each other. They mentioned the wisdom, energy, resistance, positivity, and international perspective that different students brought into the space. They acknowledged places where they found their learning enriched and challenged by their classmates. They mentioned how even when some classmates might be doing a completely different dance or not dancing at all, they figured out how to appreciate it.

We continued discussion as I threw out more conscious questions about the difference between cultural appreciation, cultural understanding, and cultural appropriation/exploitation. We asked questions about appreciating diversity and what it means to honor and appreciate a culture without having to actually do their dance. We continued as we discussed cultural and community rules, morals and ethics that are both implicit and explicit and how one navigates those spaces. We realized that these differed among the students and asked questions about how to navigate that space or refuse its influence.

Through the womanish mode of play of line dancing we were able to engage the complexity of culture and community through conscious questioning and God-given creative and collaborative imagining. And it was glorious!

PART THREE

Weaving:

Spinning the Fibers

Chapter 9

Gathering the Fibers

Play is often viewed as childish. However, what if that were conceived as a good and desirable thing for adults and not one to shy away from or even feel guilty about? In our society, we have come to view seriousness as an adult to be the norm that leads to success. Play is segregated to the children who have the freedom from adult responsibilities, bills, and a desire for achievement, and notoriety. What if we took Jesus's words to heart? "Unless you change and become like children, you will never enter the kingdom of heaven" (Matt. 18:3). What if we gave real thought and consideration to what it means to become like a child? According to Jerome Berryman, the founder of a Montessori approach to Sunday school called *Godly Play*, Jesus's "becoming-like-a-child aphorism . . . shatters the hope of entering a state of perfection, which was longed for in ancient times and by all of us at some time. In contrast, Jesus said that life is neither just becoming nor just being. It is living in the continuing creativity of the kingdom."[1]

As adults we are often in the process of becoming something else, working for something more, or being complacent, but are we really living physically, intellectually, emotionally, and developmentally in the kin-dom of God? Could we imagine being in a world where we were not striving for a "state of perfection" but "living in the continuing creativity of the kingdom"? Faithful to its biblical meaning, Berryman is referring to the kingdom of God as more than just a

1. Jerome Berryman, *Becoming Like a Child: The Curiosity of Maturity beyond the Norm* (New York: Church, 2017), 23–24.

place but a mindset and a way of life.[2] What would it look like to be fully a child and fully an adult in action and in mentality? As scary as this thought may be for some, just imagine how life-giving it could be as well. To be fully a child and fully an adult is to have adult responsibilities and desires and yet still be open to imagination, curiosity, wonder, learning, growing, and all the surprises of life that childhood inspires and evokes. It is with this mindset that we can begin to learn and treat each other with more care and compassion as we relate to one another with openness, inclusivity, inquisitiveness, and awe.

Play is a part of what it means to be human. It is an embodied aesthetic experience and a cultural expression, which is my unique contribution to this larger conversation about play. It functions as a way of knowing, being, communicating, and making meaning. Play offers all who engage in it an opportunity to resist the fantastic hegemonic imagination[3] that promotes and praises the tightrope. I propose an understanding of play as a part of what it means to be human and an expression of one's culture and ontology—one's own being as it operates as a means of coming to know and make meaning.

Prior to defining and offering up a theology and characteristics of play, I must assert that play is truly known through felt sense and experience. Words and explanations are merely attempts to explain a phenomenon that is ultimately beyond words. As most people would understand play—you know it when you do it and see it—often the explanation of it takes some of the joy and fun out of it. It is with this acknowledgment that I attempt to put this felt sense and experience into words for the sake of consistency, clarity, and understanding throughout this book.

2. Jerome Berryman, *Godly Play: An Imaginative Approach to Religious Education* (Minneapolis: Augsburg Fortress, 1991), 8.

3. Emilie M. Townes, *Womanist Ethics and the Cultural Production of Evil* (New York: Palgrave Macmillan, 2006), 7. This is a reference made in part 1. The "fantastic hegemonic imagination" is a type of consciousness and thinking that persists until an entire society believes that the dominant group is indeed in control and the subordinate group should be oppressed and viewed as less worthy, less human.

In part 3, play, playing, and playfulness are used interchangeably. In the definition I offer, I will develop and consider play as part of our nature as human beings, an embodied aesthetic experience, and a cultural expression that is part of one's ontology and epistemology. *Play* functions as a medium for one to become socialized, make meaning, and enact agency to form one's identity in the world. *Playing* will refer to play in action while *playful* and *playfulness* will be used to describe a human trait or behavior.

As you read, I invite you to embrace this image of being "fully a child and fully an adult at the same time."[4] I invite you to be an adult who welcomes and allows wonderment, creativity, and awe to infuse your life both in action and thought as you read and think about play. I invite you to remember the way in which we have all been created by a creative creator to create . . . and play.

I begin with the work of Hungarian American psychologist Mihaly Csikszentmihalyi, who presents us with the concept of flow and the intrinsic rewards involved in play. In his work, flow is understood as "the wholistic sensation present when we act with total involvement."[5] For flow to happen, there has to be complete participation and a balanced connection between the amount of challenge or action opportunity and the skill or capability needed for a given activity or action.[6] This means that for one to enter a flow state the level of challenge and skill must be balanced. If one is not challenged enough or does not have enough skill to complete a task, the flow state cannot be entered. If there is not enough challenge or actionable opportunity,

---

4. Berryman, *Becoming Like a Child*, 39.

5. Mihaly Csikszentmihalyi, "Play and Intrinsic Rewards," *Journal of Humanistic Psychology* 15, no. 3 (July 1975): 43.

6. Csikszentmihalyi, "Play and Intrinsic Rewards," 56: "When action opportunities are perceived by the actor to overwhelm his capabilities, the resulting stress is experienced as anxiety. When the ratio of capabilities is higher, the experience is worrying. The state of flow is felt when opportunities for action are in balance with the actor's skills. The experience is then autotelic. When skills are greater than opportunities for using them, the state of boredom results, which again fades into anxiety when the ratio becomes too large." Hereafter, references to this source will appear in the text.

then the task becomes boring and the person will lose interest. If the necessary skill level is too high, then the person will become anxious and also lose interest. There must be the right balance of challenge and skill level. Csikszentmihalyi considers play a kind of "flow experience" (34). In such an experience there must be a merging of action and awareness (45–47), loss of ego (49), rules (48), and its "autotelic" nature. Autotelic nature means that one must be present and acting within a set of rules that allows for the release of one's ego and has a purpose in itself (53–54). Play as flow experience allows individuals to be whole, creative, and free without needing any other goals or rewards other than the play-flow experience itself.

This view of play raises questions about what to do with flow experiences that do not offer an intrinsic reward because there is no balance between the amount of challenge and the capability for a given action or experience. This could especially be problematic within a religious context, for instance, during a Bible study, if it "fails to provide clearly detailed activities in which the faithful can participate with the understanding that in so doing they are meeting the challenges of life" (61). It falls on the religious system to provide detailed activities in which the faithful persons can participate and make meaning of their lives within the religious community. According to Csikszentmihalyi, as long as there is a balance between the amount of challenge and the amount of skill used, then there can be play.

Psychologists and fun theorists Gina Kemp, Melinda Smith, Bernie DeKoven, and Jeanne Segal assert that humans were born to play. Play is part of our nature as human beings trying to "survive and thrive" in this world.[7] Play is considered fundamental to our very existence and is necessary as it stimulates both the body and the brain. It is through play and playing with others that trust and deep relationships can be formed. Play reveals what psychoan-

7. G. Kemp, M. Smith, B. DeKoven, and J. Segal, "Play, Creativity, and Life-long Learning: Why Play Matters for Both Kids and Adults," 2011, https://wild catcounseling.wordpress.com/wp-content/uploads/2012/05/play-creativity-and -learning_-why-play-matters-for-kids-and-adults.pdf.

alyst D. W. Winnicott would refer to as one's "true self." Winnicott notes that "the True Self comes from the aliveness of the body tissues and the working of body-functions, including the heart's action and breathing."[8] The very nature of one's aliveness is where one's true self comes from. Berryman asserts that play

is a place where one can be not only with the true self but also with the true self of others. Moreover, it is a place that also includes being with the earth and with the Creator God. Godly play, then, is not just for children. It gives us at any age room to make discoveries about a whole web of relationships—with self, others, nature, and God—to nourish us all our life. The quest for this larger reality continues all life long, but the answer does not come to us as a *product* of this creativity. It comes to us as the *process* of the creating itself.[9]

Being alive and in relationship are essential for play and healthy human living as one is living into one's true self. Playing brings us back to our true self when the busyness of life might make us forget.

Evolving from the concept of play to playfulness, the work of psychologists René Proyer and Willibald Ruch is insightful. Their work is based on the predisposition in adults to play, also known as playfulness.[10] In their work, playfulness is associated with one having good character, with morals and integrity, and it encompasses five facets: spontaneity, expressiveness, creativity, fun, and silliness.[11] These facets allow for adults to encounter and engage in life with excitement, spontaneity, and energy. This type of playfulness in adult behavior is often "predicted by humor, the appreciation of beauty and

8. D. W. Winnicott, *The Maturational Processes and the Facilitating Environment: Studies in the Theory of Emotional Development* (New York: International Universities Press, 1965), 148-49.

9. Berryman, *Godly Play*, 11-12.

10. René T. Proyer and Willibald Ruch, "The Virtuousness of Adult Playfulness: The Relation of Playfulness with Strengths of Character," *Psychology of Well-Being: Theory, Research and Practice* 1, no. 4 (October 2011): 1.

11. Proyer and Ruch, "Virtuousness of Adult Playfulness," 1.

excellence, low prudence, creativity, and teamwork."[12] This type of behavior is considered to bring about joy, new ideas, positive emotions, release stress and stimulate thinking and learning. According to Proyer and Ruch this notion of playfulness engenders positive behavior, learning, thinking, and good character in those persons that practice it.

Lastly, I refer to organization and management specialists Mary Ann Glynn and Jane Webster's "Adult Playfulness Scale." In this scale, playfulness is viewed as "an individual trait, a propensity to define (or redefine) an activity in an imaginative, nonserious or metaphoric manner so as to enhance intrinsic enjoyment, involvement, and satisfaction. Playfulness is a multidimensional construct, encompassing cognitive, affective, and behavioral components, which together constitute a continuum along which individuals range from low to high."[13] Here one views playfulness, not only as a personal trait that people have and can possibly cultivate, but also as a trait that affects all aspects of learning and being. The factors on this scale are spontaneity, expressiveness, fun, creativity, and silliness. The results of this study show that in the area of task evaluations, involvement, and performance there is a positive correlation with playfulness.[14] The results also showed that individuals who are considered playful have higher cognitive creativity and spontaneity.[15] Therefore, the results of this work suggest that playfulness has a positive correlation to cognitive learning and thinking and the carrying out and evaluating of tasks.

There are both commonalities and variations among the scholars, and one thing that all these studies have in common is the need for more research in this area. While these studies are a great start, there is much more work to be done in looking at the effects of play in the lives of adults.

12. Proyer and Ruch, "Virtuousness of Adult Playfulness," 1.
13. Mary Ann Glynn and Jane Webster, "The Adult Playfulness Scale: An Initial Assessment," *Psychological Reports* 71, no. 1 (August 1992): 85.
14. Glynn and Webster, "Adult Playfulness Scale," 93.
15. Glynn and Webster, "Adult Playfulness Scale," 98.

This literature offers a foundation of play by outlining and suggesting the importance of play for healthy human living. While all of this work is crucial for understanding play at a foundational level, I find that they still miss the mark when contemplating a more robust and inclusive understanding of play that would make space for a womanist consciousness. Indeed, flow is a concept that is closely related to play. However, Mihaly Csikszentmihalyi's focus on the balance between challenge and skill level still leaves individuals on the margins. If one does not have the skill to balance the challenge of a given activity, then they will never be able to reach a flow state. This is a problem as persons of all skill levels and abilities need to play with other persons with various skill levels and abilities to grow and develop. This brings forth learning and growth for the entire community, more so than finding oneself in a flow state—alone.

Kemp, Smith, DeKoven, and Segal rightly see play as part of our nature of trying to "survive and thrive"[16] in this world. Proyer and Ruch speak to playfulness and adult behavior and Glynn and Webster speak to playfulness and its impact on one's cognitive, developmental, and affective well-being. This is true for all human beings and these cognitive, developmental, and affective impacts on one's well-being take on different meanings for those with minoritized identities. Indeed, play is needed to help develop the brain and body, and yet there are those who have historically (and presently) had to hide their play or playful self in order to survive in this country. For some, their playfulness can be seen as a liability, lack of professionalism, or even naivete. This reality for minorities brings a new realness to what it means to "survive and thrive"[17] that these authors did not fully address in their work. In this book, I provide a more robust and inclusive definition and understanding of play that takes into account the historical and present social and cultural realities of all people, especially Black women.

16. Kemp, Smith, DeKoven, and Segal, "Play, Creativity, and Lifelong Learning," 1.
17. Kemp, Smith, DeKoven, and Segal, "Play, Creativity, and Lifelong Learning," 1.

What Is Play?

I propose a definition that promotes an inclusive understanding of play that is informed by my womanist consciousness. This definition both advances and departs from prevailing understandings of play. My definition of play involves a variety of ideas and concepts from various scholars. Each of the parts are needed to see and understand the bigger picture. This definition requires aspects of psychiatry and internal/clinical research, culture, history, behavior, ontology, aesthetics, body, and mind to substantiate a more inclusive understanding of play that makes space for a womanist consciousness, as one has yet to be provided. My definition involves four parts. The first part involves the play process and characteristics. I draw on (1) Stuart Brown's seven properties of play, (2) Scott Eberle's six elements of play, (3) Johan Huizinga's connection of culture and play, and (4) Courtney Goto's characteristics of play. Each of these authors, in their descriptions of the characteristics of play, explore the many ways in which play can function such as: a way of knowing, communicating, making meaning, and understanding God, self, and the other. Play functions as a way to build trust, relationships, and community, to bring forth the true self, and to contribute to one's cognitive and affective well-being. Play becomes a vehicle of renewal and rejuvenation, a space for the enacting of agency and moral and ethical formation. Play can become an act of liberation.

Play Properties

Stuart Brown, psychiatrist and founder of the National Institute for Play, states, "When we play, we are engaged in the purest expression of our humanity, the truest expression of our individuality."[18] He asserts, and I agree, that play is at the very core of our being and one of

18. Stuart Brown, *Play: How It Shapes the Brain, Opens the Imagination, and Invigorates the Soul* (New York: Penguin Group, 2009), 5. Henceforth, references to this source will appear in the text.

the ways in which we express our truth and our very personhood. In order to explain what makes play so integral to our humanity Brown offers seven properties of play: apparently purposeless, voluntary, inherent attraction, freedom from time, diminished consciousness of self, improvisational potential, and continuation desire (17). These properties illustrate how Brown views play as a process that evokes truth and is a necessity of life (5, 12).

In analyzing Brown's seven properties (or qualities) of play we begin with *apparent purposelessness*. This is often how play is viewed, without any particular purpose, which is why many adults view play as a waste of time. However, upon further reflection Brown notes how play is not purposeless after all and aids in stimulating the body and the brain. He also reveals how play can serve as "practice for skills in the future" (31). Often one learns and practices skills of relationship building and conflict resolution through play for future careers and life as an adult.

The second quality Brown mentions is that play is *voluntary*. This means that play is not an obligation that is forced, but an act that is done freely. In order to communicate what is at one's core, play cannot be forced or required, but must happen organically when one chooses to do so—also known as enacting agency. For me it is important to note that students in my classes always have an option. If they do not desire to play, they can witness the play and speak to what they saw and experienced that way. There is always an option.

The third property is *inherent attraction*. Play is fun, exciting, and attractive; it is something that is appealing to engage in. It makes one excited because it can physically, mentally, and emotionally increase one's mood, thought process, and productivity. I will add a personal note here that I think that we, in the United States, overproduce in an unhealthy way. I think we need a real theology of failure partnered with a healthier understanding of what productivity can mean, with the understanding that we are always more than what we produce.

Brown's fourth property is *freedom from time*. Freedom from time is that moment when one becomes so immersed in play that the passing of time is not even noticed, only the experience of playing. Play engulfs the person within the experience of playing. It is during this time that one encounters the fifth play property: *diminished consciousness of self*. In this state one no longer worries about what they look like or whether they are intelligent or ignorant. We enter a place where we "stop thinking about the fact that we are thinking" (Brown, 37), and we just play.

Once one is in this place, one encounters the sixth property of play, *improvisational potential*. This property is what allows the play to curate space for flexibility, improvisation, and spontaneity. As psychoanalyst D. W. Winnicott declares, "The spontaneous gesture is the True Self in action. Only the True Self can be creative and only the True Self can feel real."[19] It is in this improvisational space that one "stumbles upon new behaviors, thoughts, strategies, movements, or ways of being" (Brown, 18). This property of play allows one to feel more comfortable, to take risks, and to try something new, allowing one's cognitive and affective ways of being and thinking to be expanded and stretched in new and creative ways.

Brown's last play property is *continuation of desire*, which is the desire to keep the play experience going. Playing invites more playing. When experiencing play there is a sense of wanting that experience to continue. This desire to continue play invites creativity and innovation to keep the play going in the face of something that might try to end it. These seven properties allow play to bring out one's inner core truth and make play the essence of freedom.

Play is natural to all human beings and should be part of our everyday living that allows for people to have quality relationships and to be more well-rounded, healthy, and whole human beings. My understanding and definition of play, stemming from my womanist understanding, is a more inclusive type of play that promotes unity over unhealthy competition and strives for the betterment not just of the person, but also of the entire community. This unity and caring for community is one of the tenets of womanism. It is through this unity in play and playing with others that trust and deep relationships can be formed. Both trust and relationships can be dismantled by unhealthy competition. Therefore, an inclusive understanding of play

19. Winnicott, *Maturational Processes*, 148.

used in this work cannot include unhealthy competition. Unhealthy competition is the kind of competition that is not facilitated by rules and can descend into angry anarchy. This unhealthy competition can be unsafe and potentially incite violence and division instead of leading to the goal of unity. While healthy competition has rules, such as a competitive game of spades, it also has the potential to lead to unwanted outcomes; this is less likely to happen when the rules are fair and enforced to protect players and the game.

Rules and boundaries are a necessity for healthy competition and learning. Theologian Lincoln Harvey considers play an expression of freedom within a set of rules.[20] It is because of fair rules that unhealthy competition can be prevented and individuals can feel more willing to risk and play because they know they are doing it within a set of boundaries that provide a level of physical safety. Historian Johan Huizinga concurs that it is within a rules framework that true play can take place.[21] Robin Stockitt fleshes out Huizinga's thoughts by stating that, "within that scaffolding of agreed conventions, improvisation and creativity can be free to roam. Play is held therefore in a careful balance of freedom and restraint."[22] It may seem almost contradictory that boundaries make a space more freeing, but in this case they are imperative.

There is similar reasoning for rules in play as with people's need for routine in the classroom and at home. One would assume that spontaneity would encourage creativity, but it is often the opposite. Educators encourage creativity and development by taking away as many extraneous variables as possible so that the student is not distracted by the multiplicity of choices and can spend their energy exploring and learning within the parameters provided. Such space offers necessary boundaries and rules, which "hold the space together"[23] so that people can feel, think, reflect, and then act.

20. Lincoln Harvey, *A Brief Theology of Sport* (London: SCM, 2014), 64.

21. Johan Huizinga, *Homo Ludens: A Study of the Play Element in Culture* (Boston: Beacon, 1950), 28.

22. Robin Stockitt, *Imagination and the Playfulness of God* (Eugene, OR: Pickwick, 2011), 102.

23. Alice Y. Kolb and David A. Kolb, "Learning to Play, Playing to Learn:

Specifically looking at the ludic learning space, "a holistic model that views play and learning as a unified and integral process of human learning and development,"[24] play is given the freedom to create deep learning—physically, mentally, spiritually, and morally within adults. This type of experience stimulates the brain and the body, as persons begin to see this as a way of coming to know who they are and how they are in relationship with the other. Play builds trust and relationships through unity and teamwork that engenders questions of ethics and morality of how to play and be in community.

Organizational behaviorists Alice Y. Kolb and David A. Kolb provide us with an example of an intramural softball league that started on a university campus.[25] The league started as a very competitive league, but everyone did not agree with or enjoy playing in such a competitive and aggressive manner. As a result, they decided to form their own league where anyone could come and go as they pleased and play for the fun of the game. This brought to the surface people's ethical values and ideals of fair play. Kolb and Kolb quote Huizinga when he states that this league "puts to the test the player's ethical values of courage, resilience, and most importantly, 'fairness.'"[26] They had a set day and time that they would play every week and they would play with whoever showed up. This gave their play boundaries. They learned to express themselves and their feelings, build community, play fair, temper their sense of aggression and competition, and enjoy a shared experience with a group of people.

Many of the players confirmed that they had grown and learned a great deal about themselves and each other since the start of the league. One person even commented that in this team he found his "family."[27] Play offers this type of learning, growing, relationship building, and developing that aid in an individual's cognitive and affective well-being in a playful way. Play offers this type of experience

---

A Case Study of a Ludic Learning Space," *Journal of Organizational Change Management* 23, no. 1 (2010): 45.

24. Kolb and Kolb, "Learning to Play," 27.
25. Kolb and Kolb, "Learning to Play," 31.
26. Kolb and Kolb, "Learning to Play," 43.
27. Kolb and Kolb, "Learning to Play," 42.

for all who choose to play within boundaries, without unhealthy competition and aggressive agendas.

The Play Process

Given the properties of play that Brown has provided, one might find oneself going through a particular process in order to benefit from all the various properties that play entails. The vice president for play studies and editor of *The American Journal of Play*, Scott Eberle provides a six-step play process that is voluntary and driven by "pleasure that yet strengthens our muscles, instructs our social skills, tempers and deepens our positive emotions, and enables a state of balance that leaves us poised."[28] Such play makes us better cognitively and affectively as we play through various situations and issues that arise. Not every player goes through every step of this process, but these are the elements that are involved when one plays. Eberle uses these six elements—anticipation, surprise, pleasure, understanding, strength and poise—as components within the process of play (222). In his article, Eberle provides a chart that shows each of these six elements including the various dimensions, or "expressions" (which grow in intensity as one progresses), of each (221). Although this seems linear, the process of play and reaching various dimensions within the elements of play is a fluid one that encompasses much ebb and flow, reflecting Brown's play properties.

Eberle's first element of play is *anticipation*. Because one is never sure what will happen when one plays, there is a level of uncertainty and risk that is involved so that the player awaits with curiosity, expectation, and even sometimes, anxiety. As Eberle states, anticipation is "an imaginative, predictive, pleasurable tension" (222). This is the delightful giddiness that one feels, not knowing what will happen but looking forward to the possibilities. "Interest" and "wonderment" are two aspects, or expressions, of anticipation that Eberle

28. Scott G. Eberle, "The Elements of Play," *American Journal of Play* 6, no. 2 (2014): 231. Hereafter, references to this source will appear in the text.

provides (221). Anticipation can lead to *surprise*. Play leads to discovery with new ideas and thoughts that are unpredictable. These new perspectives and shifts in thought are often surprising to encounter. While this element may start with surprise, the more one plays, the more one begins to experience appreciation and even astonishment (221).

The surprise of play can produce the next element: *pleasure*. The players receive pleasure in the surprises that play brings. They feel joy, happiness, and a sense of excitement and positivity while playing, which is often pleasurable. They experience this pleasure at different levels, depending on their participation in the play. Eberle lists "satisfaction" and "fun" as happenings during the onset of play and pleasure as an outcome of extended playing (221). Pleasure is motivation to continue playing because it is a desirable feeling to experience. This can engender *understanding*.

During play one discovers various ways of thinking and knowing with a potential shift in perspective. Eberle says that play "delivers emotional and intellectual bonuses—enlarging both our talent for empathy and our capacity for insight" (224). Play allows one to grow cognitively as one begins to think differently and understand various insights in new ways. Eberle lists "tolerance" as a starting place with "mastery" coming with more time, understanding, and experience playing (221). Understanding during play can develop *strength*—both physical and emotional. This strength comes from knowing and understanding more about oneself, others, and the world. Strength here refers to both strength of mind and body (225). This strength comes through the form of controlling and mastering a particular skill or task. This involves endurance and innovation. Eberle offers "stamina" as the starting place with "creativity" being a possible outcome with more time playing (221). The benefit and result of having understanding and strength is *poise*. Poise involves a balanced level of fulfillment that is a reward to the player who encounters all these play elements by engaging in this process.

If we think of this process as circular, each element is ready to begin once another element has been reached. It is important to remember that this is a fluid and dynamic play process that ebbs and flows between these elements at any given time; a player should not feel that they must complete them in sequence, for they will organically happen.

Culture and Play Connection

One of the unique contributions of my present work is the view of play as a cultural expression. I have discussed Kathryn Tanner's notion of culture, and to encompass a more inclusive and womanist idea of play, culture must be explored even further. While many mention the importance and link between play and culture, I make the claim that play is indeed a cultural expression. It is also important to note that play properties and the elements of the play process will vary among cultures. Different cultures play differently as a matter of their own historical realities, resources, and learned behavior as a cultural group. Cultural historian Johan Huizinga proposes that cultures have evolved through various forms of play, and therefore play should be viewed as culturally particular.[29] I agree that there is a cultural dimension to play since each person is born into a culture that affects how they view themselves and their world and how they play. I discussed the specifics of play as cultural expression through womanism in part 2.

Huizinga asserts that human beings should not only be seen as *Homo Sapiens* but also *Homo Ludens* or "human who plays," since play is a large part of what makes us human. Huizinga believes that play is a way in which to live life and to make meaning of life.[30] I concur with Huizinga's thoughts around culture and play. As play is a way in which a person has being and lives out their core religious morals, values, and truths, it is naturally affected by one's cultural history and experience. History, gender, class, social location, ability, geographic location, and other variables affect one's culture, community, and experience—and thus one's play.

29. Huizinga, *Homo Ludens*, ix.
30. Huizinga, *Homo Ludens*, ix.

For example, because of the experience of slavery and oppression of African Americans, their idea of play will differ from that of an Anglo-Saxon male, whose family owned slaves; these differing perspectives endure across later generations. Originally, the Anglo-Saxon male may have had more access to various toys, trinkets, paintbrushes, and other play instruments than the African American woman. She might identify more with bodily play as she is aware of her body since she uses it frequently to plow fields and to work hard with her hands and body. This African American woman may experience bodily play in the form of dance as she expresses her very being and ways of knowing through the movement of her body. This does not place importance of one over the other; it simply means their methods and elements in the play process may look different for these two individuals from different cultures. This does not mean that play is not equally important because it looks different; it just means that one must consider culture during play and when playing with others.

To think even further about what this might look like within a particular context, I turn to religious educator Courtney Goto, who has developed Local Practical Theological Aesthetics (LPTA). LPTA "speaks of and to the community by appealing to people's particular sensual preferences, their context, and their way of being in the world."[31] It helps one consider how faith communities such as churches or theological classrooms look different depending on one's community, context, and culture. She mentions how one's "faith community impacts how teaching is experienced in the body and how what is taught conveys meanings that go beyond words" (108). Since play is relational and often involves others, playing does not just impact one single person, but it ripples like a rock hitting the water. When the rock hits the water, it flows out for a distance. Just as when one person is affected, those within closest proximity feel it and it moves outward into the community. The opposite is also true as the

31. Courtney T. Goto, *The Grace of Playing: Pedagogies for Leaning into God's New Creation* (Eugene, OR: Pickwick, 2016), 109. Hereafter, references to this source will appear in the text.

community and culture that a person is from affects the person. It is a reciprocal relationship that enriches, teaches, and challenges the person, community, and culture.

Play Characteristics

Play and playing are tools of the mind and the body that allow for agency and liberation. Play is fun, voluntary, transcendent, exciting, creative, humorous, joyful, and surprising. Play instructs our social skills, deepens our emotions, enhances our cognitive functioning, brings joy, makes space for lament and grief, and encourages moral formation. Religious educator Courtney Goto offers three specific characteristics of play: "losing and finding oneself"; "acting or believing 'as if'"; and entering "a world of possibilities" (15-16). She explains her notion of "losing and finding" oneself as "important to the meanings of playing by bringing to mind a familiar experience. . . . A player can lose herself in the experience of playing, yet strangely she can emerge with the sense of being 'found.'. . . Something hidden comes to light. . . . Some thinkers have noted the possibility of experiencing transcendence while playing, in the sense of finding oneself in the midst of something larger than oneself" (16).

Here I am brought back to the works of Mihaly Csikszentmihalyi and Stuart Brown as they both noted the importance of the experience of losing time or entering a flow state while experiencing play. This sense of timelessness and experiencing transcendence while playing is one of its gifts and key characteristics.

Goto's third play characteristic is entering a world of possibilities. In this world "playing ignites the senses and imagination as possibilities emerge, fall away, are reborn, and change—sometimes quixotically moment by moment, other times with subtlety, strategy, or deliberation" (17). This characteristic is important as it makes space for creativity, imagination, and embodiment. This characteristic of play allows for agency as one can create something new and imagine something more than what there might be in the current moment. This can often be revelatory in life and faith.

Goto's third characteristic goes hand in hand with the second through acting and believing "as if." Goto asserts that acting and believing "as if" "allows a person to sense what is authentic or real by inviting the player to enter a fictive world. Acting or believing 'as if' entails setting aside enough disbelief, appearances, or literal ways of thinking to shift temporarily into another way of engaging reality and one another" (16). This allows one to see another perspective, think outside one's self and truly begin to see the other. This refers to the work of Jerome Berryman and D. W. Winnicott about the "true self." For Goto and Berryman it is this experience of acting and believing "as if" that "is a place where one can be with one's true self and the true self of others."[32] In this space we can be ourselves, without judgment of what society might think or say. This place of truth and trust is integral during play.

32. Berryman, *Godly Play*, 11.

Chapter 10

The Forgotten Strand

I now present an important but often forgotten strand of my play. Everything that has been mentioned thus far that play is and engenders would not be possible without both the mind and the *body*. There is a science to the movement of the body that must be addressed here. Kinesiology, deriving from the Greek words *kinein* (to move) and *kinesis* (movement), is the study of the function and mechanics of body movement or human motion. It "is based on a knowledge of the anatomy and physiology of the neuromusculoskeletal system and the physical laws of force, motion, and gravity."[1] The mind is essential as it sends information to the rest of the body to move and to do various things. The body is vital within the work of play as it is what the mind moves in various ways that create emotions, fun, energy, moral formation, agency, and cognitive development. It is often one's body that is engaged in the play process—through movement.

In order for play to happen, there must be an equal partnership—a double Dutch of sorts—of the mind and body, not the dualism or hierarchy of the two that is rampant in the academy. The mind needs the body and the body needs the mind. When trying to move or play, it is the brain that must make the decision about which muscles need to contract to get a particular part of the body to do a particular thing. Simultaneously, the brain must also try to estimate how much force or resistance is needed to hold, pick up, or drop a particular object. Then, there is also the consideration of external factors like the

1. Marion R. Broer, *An Introduction to Kinesiology* (Hoboken, NJ: Prentice-Hall, 1968), vii.

weather when doing the movement or the material of a particular object. For example, if someone is throwing a basketball to a friend, her brain must send messages to the muscles in her body that would be involved in throwing the ball. Her arms, elbows, and wrists would need to be involved to throw a ball. However, if she is throwing the ball a longer distance to someone who is much taller than her, she might need to move her legs and abdomen to be able to push the ball out with greater force. Her mind, specifically her primary motor cortex, is responsible for generating the neural impulses or "signals that control the execution of movement."[2]

The mind sends signals to make the body move, but what motivates the neural impulses and signals? Marion R. Broer shares the motivation: "To understand human movement, one must understand not only the ways in which the body can move or be moved and the laws that govern efficient movement, but also the ways in which the human being is motivated to move and the effects this motion has on the total person—his body (mechanically and physiologically), his emotions, and his concepts concerning himself and his environment."[3]

To reiterate what Broer is saying, movement is a cyclical total person experience. The body feels sensations and emotions through movement and motion that are sent to the brain. The brain is then motivated by those sensations, thoughts, and emotions to send signals that move the body in particular ways. Health and physical education teacher Traci L. Lengel and academic director of the Regional Training Center Mike Kuczala state it well when they say that the body and the brain "have been mistakenly assumed as separate entities. The fact is that they flow to and through each other, as an extension and a reflection of the other's will."[4] They need each other and are reflections of each other, all

---

2. Eric Jensen, *Teaching with the Brain in Mind*, 2nd ed. (Alexandria, VA: Association for Supervision and Curriculum Development, 2005).

3. Broer, *Introduction to Kinesiology*, 1.

4. Traci Lengel and Mike Kuczala, *The Kinesthetic Classroom: Teaching and Learning Through Movement* (Thousand Oaks, CA: Corwin, 2010), 16.

wrapped up in a beautiful blood and skin package playing double Dutch all the time.

The brain and body connection is important in this work as I am specifically advocating for play in the theological classroom. I am advocating for this kind of holistic teaching and learning that involves the entire person—mind and body. The mind is often valued and praised over the body within the academy. However, Lengel and Kuczala use Harvard associate clinical professor of psychiatry John Ratey's description of movement and exercise as "Miracle-Gro" for brain development.[5] Lengel and Kuczala lay out what movement does for a person in the classroom. Movement allows a break or rest period for individuals to refocus and come back with new thoughts, ideas, and perspectives. Movement allows for more implicit learning to take place. This learning goes beyond what one may consciously be aware of at the moment. Take, for example, riding a bike. Once one learns the movements of riding a bike it becomes second nature—happening without even thinking about it.[6] Movement improves the function in the brain by allowing and creating a space or environment for neurogenesis—creation of new neurons and brain cells—to occur, which engenders new learning.[7] These new connections in the mind and the body explain things like muscle memory when riding the bike or driving home from work physically without even remembering it. Our bodies hold these memories and knowledge within them that the mind needs. These are just a few of the benefits of the mind and body connection that are developed and lived out through play.

Play allows for what Marilyn Patterson calls the "bodymind." "The mind plays a major role in the health of the body, and the body, in turn, helps determine how effectively the mind works. Many scientists are now beginning to think in terms of the 'bodymind,' a unity that many traditional cultures have never lost. Serving as a bridge between the body and mind, the kinesthetic aspect of the bodily

5. Lengel and Kuczala, *Kinesthetic Classroom*, 17.
6. Lengel and Kuczala, *Kinesthetic Classroom*, 23-24.
7. Lengel and Kuczala, *Kinesthetic Classroom*, 25-26.

kinesthetic intelligence lets us receive and interpret the millions of signals, both internal and external, that keep us alive."[8] Our entire person needs every part of us to play, to think and to be in this world. Because they are linked, all movement is also a sensorimotor experience, which means that the physical movement of the body affects the cognitive and affective happenings and development of the brain and vice versa.[9] It is this kind of "bodymind" connection that play engenders. Play functions as a method or tool for cognitive and affective development, moral and ethical formation, problem solving, exploration, team building, and space to enact agency and push for liberation. This play is not only important and vital for children, but adults as well.

8. Marilyn Nikimaa Patterson, *Every Body Can Learn: Engaging the Bodily-Kinesthetic Intelligence in the Everyday Classroom* (Tucson, AZ: Zephyr Press, 1997), 4.

9. Broer, *Introduction to Kinesiology*, 8.

Chapter 11

Twisting the Strands

In Hans-Georg Gadamer's seminal work, *Truth and Method*, he writes of "the ontology of the work of art and its hermeneutic significance." Gadamer believes play to be a mode of existing and being in the world, affirming my prior assertions by Stuart Brown and others that play is a part of human nature. As Gadamer asserts, play is "the mode of being of the work of art itself." For Gadamer, play gives clues to ontological explanation in that play is completely experience based: "It becomes an experience that changes the person who experiences it."[1] Part of what makes play, *play*, is experiencing it. One begins to see play as its own entity with structure and order that can take over and engulf a person through the experience of finding and losing oneself. This experience can engulf a person because it is a natural process that is part of "pure self-presentation."[2] For Gadamer play is a way of being, of presenting oneself, and existing in the world. Using Gadamer's definition, play involves, but is not exclusive to art, games, drama, sports, music, dance, double Dutch, etc. These types of play involve what Gadamer calls movement of "backward and forward." This movement is exactly as it sounds, the moving of one's body and mind forward and backward. It is in the continual back and forth that one is moving, playing, and jumping with ideas, possibilities, and concepts. This movement is essential in exploring oneself, the world, and the Divine. This movement of going back and then mov-

1. Hans-Georg Gadamer, *Truth and Method* (New York: Bloomsbury, 1975), 102-3.
2. Gadamer, *Truth and Method*, 105.

ing forward, or moving forward and then moving backward, allows one to experience agency and decide one's own behaviors, morals, and values, which are incorporated in moving forward and backward. In this back and forth one is renewed as play "renews itself in constant repetition."[3]

Aesthetic Experience as an Aspect of Theological Anthropology

Aesthetic experience as an aspect of theological anthropology begins by defining theological anthropology and aesthetic experience. I must clarify that in this work there is a preference to theological aesthetics. Theological anthropology looks at the human person as it relates to God and the Divine. Echoing the first biblical account of creation, theologian Sallie McFague declares that human beings are made in the image of God and can use language to speak of this divine-human relationship.[4] This divine-human relationship is further conceptualized through the work of theologian M. Shawn Copeland, who asserts that "theological anthropology seeks to understand the meaning and purpose of existence within the context of divine revelation."[5] Copeland gives three central convictions for a theological anthropology that comes from a Christian interpretation: "(1) that human beings, created in the image and likeness of God (*imago Dei*), have a distinct capacity for communion with God; (2) that human beings have a unique place in the cosmos God created; and (3) that human beings are made for communion with other living beings."[6] Being made in the image of God, having a unique place in this world, and being relational beings leads to the question of how one experi-

3. Gadamer, *Truth and Method*, 104.
4. Sallie McFague, *Metaphorical Theology: Models of God in Religious Language* (Philadelphia: Fortress, 1982), 146-47.
5. M. Shawn Copeland, *Enfleshing Freedom: Body, Race, and Being* (Minneapolis: Fortress, 2010), 23.
6. Copeland, *Enfleshing Freedom*, 24.

ences and lives out these realities. This question of how invites the definition of aesthetic experience.

Aesthetic experience is an experience that is often desirable and pleasurable as it involves the senses and gives life meaning. It is a semiotics or a meaning making through sign processes, experience, and meaningful communication. It asks the question that Alejandro García-Rivera posed, "What moves the human heart?" In the asking, it explores the variety of theological methods of interpretation as the Spirit moves freely and the Divine breathes in the movement. It allows a person's imagination to take them outside of themselves to a place where there is hope that in the beautiful and the ugly, transformation and transcendence can still be found, where truth resides, where interpretations and meaning can be made, and where life is worth living.

This definition starts with the work of late scientist, pastor, and theologian Alejandro García-Rivera of Havana, Cuba. He was the first to think about aesthetics and theology in the form of the question, "What moves the human heart?"[7] Asking this question "brings us closer to the mysterious experience of the truly beautiful, an experience that transcends geological space and prehistoric time, an experience that holds the most persuasive claim to being what has become an aporia in our day, the real universal."[8] While I must assert that in my experience, what elicits aesthetic experience is not universal, his claim is provocative. When was the last time we thought about what moves our hearts, or gave ourselves permission to let our hearts be moved? There is something powerful, mysterious, and honest in a heart being moved and I believe this is the key to aesthetic experience and what play can provide. García-Rivera draws from the work of Hans Urs von Balthasar when he claims, "Theological aesthetics recognizes in the experience of the truly beautiful a religious dimension." He speaks of a beauty that is transcendent and begins in God's Own Self and a "divine initiation" of love and we get the free choice to

7. Alejandro García-Rivera, *The Community of the Beautiful: A Theological Aesthetics* (Collegeville, MN: Liturgical Press, 1999), 9.
8. García-Rivera, *The Community of the Beautiful*, 9.

respond.[9] There is not only an action but also a response, much like that of salvation. There is to-and-fro, just as Gadamer described. God is pouring out love and one has the choice to respond to it or not. It is in the freedom that one's heart can be moved, knowing that one is not forced, but one chooses it from a place of liberation. García-Rivera puts it quite beautifully: "Theological aesthetics attempts to make clear once again the connection between Beauty and the beautiful, between Beauty's divine origins and its appropriation by the human heart. . . . Human life has a worth and a dignity which only Beauty can reveal through the beautiful. Without the language and experience of Beauty and the beautiful, the Church will find difficult the expression of her faith, much less her conviction of the dignity of the human person, and, even less, be a sacrament to the world."[10]

It is like a conversation where the whole world is important, worthy, and full of dignity and truth. It is in this mysterious and precious place that one can be free enough to let one's heart be moved. Religion professor Steven Guthrie states that "the words *ruach* and *pneuma* mean not only 'spirit,' but also 'breath' or 'wind.' Spirit, then, is a word that suggests movement and movement of an organic sort . . . it is most intimately connected to us; we could not survive apart from it, yet we cannot dictate its arrival or cessation."[11] Therefore, if one is allowing one's heart to be moved, one is allowing the Spirit to move, the divine to breathe through one, and in this allowance or human response there is freedom of the movement that is mysterious and unknown. This movement allows one to "speak languages beyond language and know truths beyond knowing."[12] It allows one the space to explore and to know one's true self.

One comes to know that what is experienced is understood and known. Gadamer believes that play is a way or mode of being in the world and it becomes known and understood through artistic

9. García-Rivera, *The Community of the Beautiful*, 9–10.

10. García-Rivera, *The Community of the Beautiful*, 11.

11. Steven R. Guthrie, *Creator Spirit: The Holy Spirit and the Art of Becoming Human* (Grand Rapids: Baker Academic, 2011), 8.

12. Guthrie, *Creator Spirit*, 8.

creativity and liberation. Play, then, is an aesthetic experience or a way in which one can ask and let one's heart be moved. Play is an aesthetic experience as it involves the senses and can provide meaning to life. Play is an aesthetic experience as it can function as a way of meaning making through experience and meaningful communication. In this way, play can form, inform, and then transform individuals and communities. It can operate as a way of knowing, being, and making meaning in the world. Play allows us to make meaning of what is real in our lives, including our given horizons and values as well as the unknown, mysterious, and the Divine. This type of play induces shared meaning with others and often engenders more play. Play, as an embodied aesthetic experience, allows for communication as a way in which we experience, come to know, have our being in the world, and find shared meaning with the other.

This type of experience and movement is like double Dutch. Double Dutch is like Gadamer's to-and-fro moving backward and forward, making meaning, coming to know, and being with self, one another, and the Divine. In this playing, all human partners are equal and interdependent and move freely between and among each other. This is much like the "divine dance" that feminist Catholic theologian Catherine Mowry LaCugna mentions in her book *God for Us*. [13] In this book LaCugna speaks of the inner life of our One and Triune God as perichoresis, "mutually permeating one another," "being-in-one-another, permeation without confusion"; "the three divine persons mutually inhere in one another, draw life from one another, 'are' what they are by relation to one another." [14] To think of the three divine persons in mutual harmony with one another in community, equality, and freedom is a beautiful vision that all persons are meant to live out and be mirrors of as beings made in the *imago Dei*.

13. Catherine Mowry LaCugna, *God for Us: The Trinity and Christian Life* (New York: HarperOne, 1991), 271. Hereafter, references to this source will appear in the text.

14. LaCugna, *God for Us*, 72, 271, 270.

We are made to be beings that jump in the perpetual to-and-fro, in the dynamic and creative energy of the creator and this world. We are made to jump with all of humanity as our "beloved partners."[15] Play is one way to jump the ropes. Play involves the movement of going backward and forward that Gadamer explained. Play involves making meaning of this mutuality, community, and freedom among us. Play is living out—movement and rope jumping (both metaphorically and literally); it is an embodied aesthetic experience that not only functions as a way we begin to make meaning in the world, come to know, but can become a way we live out our being and knowing in the world.

My Definition of Play

Play is a part of our human nature. Play is an aesthetic experience that involves the bodymind and is therefore embodied, making play an embodied aesthetic experience. We understand play to be both things, but what makes this work unique is the claim that play is also a cultural expression that functions as a way of expressing one's identity and very being in the world. Because play is a cultural expression and an embodied aesthetic experience that is part of our ontology and epistemology it functions as a way of knowing and a means for communication and meaning making. My definition of play is marked by apparent purposelessness, volunteering, attraction, freedom from time, diminished consciousness of self, improvisational potential, and continuation of desire while also maintaining a sense of unity, boundaries, and fairness. Play is constituted by anticipation, surprise, pleasure, understanding, strength, and poise while recognizing that these may vary among different cultures and communities. Play involves finding and losing self within the many possibilities of life as we are coming to know, understand, and experience our own being in the world. Play invites us into the mys-

15. LaCugna, *God for Us*, 274.

terious, beautiful, ugly, and the Divine as an aesthetic experience using both our mind and our body to express our cultural and social realities. Play invites us to practice agency and critical engagement in the world.

Play brings out our core truth or true self as well as aiding in both cognitive and affective development. Play informs us about who we are and who we want to be, then actually forms us through the practice of it, and ultimately it transforms us into persons that can communicate, cultivate relationships, and make meaning across difference. Play allows us to become socialized, make meaning, and enact agency to form our identity in the world, in light of our cultural histories and present realities. Play provides the space for each of us to think beyond what is present to the "as if" and a world of possibilities that can deepen our emotions and enhance our cognitive functioning, which encourages moral and ethical formation through fair play. Play and the action of playing are capacities of the mind and the body that are not only pleasurable, voluntary, purposeful, surprising, creative, and exciting but also allow for agency and liberation through freedom and unity with fair rules. Play instructs our social skills, deepens our emotions, enhances our cognitive functioning, holds space for joy and lament, encourages moral formation, and engenders balance by providing a space that aids in integrating the body, mind, and spirit in a way that invites exploration and risk.

Theological educator Jaco J. Hamman states that "to grow in play-fullness is almost always an act of reclamation and restoration, reclaiming a part of our lives that we lost somewhere along the road of life. Play-fullness re-humanizes us."[16] It seems wrong to not take this moment, in this chapter on play, to actually invite you, the reader, to play. So let us take a moment to reclaim, restore, and rehumanize through remembering. Remember a time when you experienced play. Take a moment to think back and remember it.

16. Jaco J. Hamman, *A Play-Full Life: Slowing Down and Seeking Peace* (Cleveland: Pilgrim, 2011), 17.

Where were you?
What were you doing?
What was the space like that invited the play?
Who were your play partners?
What emotions, attitudes or behaviors did it engender?
How did you feel before, during, and after the playing?
What did you learn from the play?

Does your experience resonate with some of what was presented and discussed in this chapter? Why or why not? What more might you dream of?

Chapter 12

Womanish Modes of Play

Embody God's Love

Here I offer part three of the womanist definition and the accompanying ethical tenet of womanism from Alice Walker and Stacey Floyd-Thomas.

> Loves music. Loves dance. Loves the moon. *Loves* the Spirit. Loves love and food and roundness. Loves struggle. *Loves* the Folk. Loves herself. *Regardless.*[1]

> By demystifying the perceptions of black women's bodies, ways, and loves as vile, the intentionality with which black women writers reconcile black women back to their truer selves is invaluable in the formation of womanist ethics . . . womanist theologian Michele Jacques notes that Walker's "call to love herself 'regardless' is one of the most foundationally holistic and revolutionary political actions African-American women can take," a call that is the hallmark of the womanist tradition.[2]

There is still a focus on the self but in relationship to embodying God's love toward oneself, creation, God, and others. When we begin with identity, heritage, culture, and history we are able to understand ourself better. A conscious understanding of self and our his-

1. Alice Walker, *In Search of Our Mothers' Gardens: Womanist Prose* (New York: Harcourt, Brace, 1983), xi–xii. Emphasis original.
2. Stacey Floyd-Thomas, *Mining the Motherlode: Methods in Womanist Ethics* (Cleveland: Pilgrim, 2006), 9–10.

tory moves us to loving self and others more fully; as God loves us. This radical kind of love involves truly embodying God's love in our heart, mind, soul, and body. This involves looking even more deeply into oneself and affirming oneself as divinely and humanly lovable. This is where womanist theological anthropology becomes essential to this work. For many Black women, our bodies have not been our own, merely seen as objects or dangerous. This has translated into self-dislike, body dysmorphia, and at times body or self-hatred. Therefore, taking the step to truly see ourself as deserving and worthy of not only self-love, but of God's love is a journey that takes time, honesty, and vulnerability. We must look at ourself and see the hurt, pain, pride, ego, past experiences and still see the beloved person that was created in the image and likeness of God. This important step takes creative and collaborative imagination to re-vision, re-claim, and re-story as needed.

Once we can see ourselves as a person of worth, dignity, and honor then it becomes a bit easier to also see the dignity, worth, and honor in others. When we can truly embody God's love for and within ourself without conditions, we are better able to express that love to, for, and with others. When we truly embody God's love for ourselves we are able to unapologetically envision, dream, act, and risk in liberating ways.

To aid participants in beginning the process of seeing themselves as divinely and humanly lovable, the educator or minister can offer womanish modes of play that enable students to look within, wrestle with themselves to resist the dominant narrative, to embrace and enact agency and autonomy in playful ways. These womanish modes of play can be, but are not limited to affirmations, reimagining Scripture, creating a vision board, and playing Jenga. An educator can utilize any of these to bring about introspection, connection, and self-discovery. These womanish modes of play encourage participants to get to know themselves and their own worth and dignity as beings made in the image and likeness of God. They invite participants to honestly reflect on themselves, the good and the bad, without blame and to resist, re-story, re-claim, and re-vision as needed. Then once we are able to name who we are we can begin to assess and know that even in the midst of our strengths and weaknesses we are still made in the image and likeness of God and loved unconditionally.

These modes of play allow participants to critically engage through conscious questioning and creative and collaborative imagining and re-visioning in order to reflect upon who we are through the eyes and heart of God. Hopefully, after these playful practices, participants will believe, as Ntozake Shange stated, "My love is too beautiful . . . too sanctified . . . too magic . . . too Saturday nite . . . too complicated . . . too music to have thrown back on my face."[3]

Essentials and Suggestions

The modes of play mentioned below curate clearing space for us to embody God's love playfully with our own thoughts and feelings, while honoring and respecting the embodied thoughts and feelings of another. When we question and reflect, we realize that we are embodied and when we see or make contact with other embodied persons, we treat them with more care. We are more inclined to set personal biases aside, offer grace, truly listen and see the other, which sometimes allows for the changing of pre-existing biases. While this is clearly the ideal, it is hard work that takes time and takes intentional effort, conscious questioning, and critical reflection from the educator or minister as well as the persons involved.

The practices below literally enable participants to look at themselves and the other. They bring awareness to the spaces where the world, society, or ourselves has claimed that we are not enough, do not deserve love, are not worthy, or are problematic in some way. These modes of play then allow for the dismantling of these "problems" by having us look at ourself as a person made in the image and likeness of God with worth, dignity, and beauty. These modes of play allow us to creatively and collaboratively imagine something more

3. Ntozake Shange, *For Colored Girls Who Have Considered Suicide When the Rainbow Is Enuf: A Choreopoem* (New York: Macmillan, 1977), 46–47.

and to begin to enact agency, re-claim, re-story, and resist oppressive and dominant narratives physically, cognitively, and affectively.

These practices are by no means easy and are quite complex and challenging for all involved. There is a level of vulnerability and trust that is required that will take time to develop. This might mean these practices should not be done upon a first meeting, but after trust has been built. In order to establish this kind of environment we need to have a clearing space in which participants feel comfortable to share, be vulnerable, be silly, and handle things that are shared with care. This might look like establishing a covenant of trust, of presence, confidentiality, or participation, being sure to make it personal and specific for the needs of the given group.

These modes of play allow one to engage with thoughts, ideas and feelings in playful bodily ways in order to begin to think about what it means to embody God's love for ourself, creation, and others. When we see, not only each other, but also ourselves as embodied individuals and not floating heads, perspectives change, love is embodied and shared, humanity is seen, and transformation can happen.

Womanish Modes of Play: Embody God's Love

- *Womanish mode of play:* One week of affirmations.
- *Materials needed:* Sticky notes or paper to write on and a writing utensil.
- *Environment/space:* A place with a flat surface to write on.
- *Directions:* After discussing the importance of embodying God's love, invite students to write and make seven affirmations, one for each day for one week. Invite them to think about who they are and what God might want them to know, think, be reminded of, or be challenged by about themselves and write that. Then invite your students to pick one random affirmation each day, to start their day and to hold with them for that day. They are to do this for the next seven days as they embody God's love for themselves.
- *Questions for reflection:*
  - How did it feel to affirm yourself every day?

- What surprised you?
- What was affirmed or confirmed within you?
- What did you learn about yourself?
- What did you learn about what it means to embody God's love for yourself?

• *Womanish mode of play:* Scripture reimagined.
• *Materials needed:* A Bible and something to write on and with.
• *Environment/space:* A place with a flat surface to read and write.
• *Directions:* After discussing the importance of embodying God's love for ourselves, invite students to revisit a piece of Scripture (e.g., Psalm 88)[4] through the lens of embodying God's love for themselves. Invite them to read the Scripture a few times, then to reimagine that same Scripture through the eyes and love of the Divine. Invite them to rewrite the Scripture through the eyes of God and think about what might need to shift or change in the Scripture if it conveyed more of God's love, grace, and kindness.
• *Questions for reflection:*
- What Scripture did you choose and why?
- How has what you read shifted and changed? Why?
- How do you feel about what you have reimagined?
- How might we offer this kind of reimagining and embodying of God's love for ourselves every day?
- What are three things you think God would want you to love more about yourself?

• *Womanish mode of play:* Curate a vision board.
• *Materials needed:* This can be done using an app online such as canva.com using the vision board template. This can also be done with poster board, magazine clippings, glue, scissors, and markers.
• *Environment/space:* A place with a flat surface to use for creating or an electronic device to use a particular creation application.
• *Directions:* After discussing the importance of embodying God's love you can invite students to create a vision board for themselves. This

---

4. This was done and inspired by one of my students: Kristi Yeatman.

can be the next 3–6 months, 1–3 years, or 5–10 years. It is really up to you as the teacher, and I would encourage you to go with what your students need and would respond well to. Whatever time frame is decided upon, the students should reflect not only on the desires they might have but also on what they think God might have for them. Remind them that God wants them to live and dream expansively, so not to play small but to really think about what God would want for them in their lives and just dream freely.

- *Questions for reflection:*
  - How did it feel to vision and dream?
  - How did it feel to put pictures and words to those dreams?
  - Who might you want to share this with and why?
  - What might be your next step to living out this vision?

- *Womanish mode of play:* Jenga.
- *Materials needed:* The game Jenga. There is a regular version that can fit on any table and there are large versions that can go on the ground.
- *Environment/space:* Space for pieces to fall and move without hurting anyone or anything.
- *Directions:* After discussing the importance of embodying God's love, invite students to play Jenga. Invite them to read and or agree upon common rules for the game and then to play together as they think about what the standing, the strategy, and falling of blocks might have to say about embodying God's love.
- *Questions for reflection:*
  - How did it feel to play Jenga?
  - What strategy did you use and why?
  - How did it feel to wonder if your move was going to make the game collapse or not?
  - When it collapsed and fell, how did you feel?

Practical Example of Embodying God's Love

While teaching a class, in order to get students to begin to embody God's love and to see their God-given worth within themselves I invited them to write seven affirmations on seven different sticky notes. I then invited them to pick a random affirmation each day for seven days as homework. They were to read the affirmation first thing in the morning and to keep what it said with them for that day and allow themselves to embody God's love for themselves.

When we discussed this homework the following week students had mixed experiences. Some students felt it was too heavy and that they were not ready to really dig into this, so they just focused on one affirmation for the whole week, which they still found helpful and affirming of God's love within them. Other students found this practice helpful and revelatory about themselves and their need to embody God's love and grace for themselves more often. One student said she was transformed by the idea that she needed to "love myself enough to give my dreams a chance."[5] Some students discussed the beauty of how they randomly picked the exact affirmation that they needed for that particular day and how that made them feel God's love and presence even more. Lastly, there were students that said they couldn't find their affirmations, to which I responded that the affirmations will find them, when they are meant to, and they have to covenant to do them for that week when they find them, and the students agreed.

As a result of this womanish mode of play, many came to new understandings and appreciations of their own places of intersection and the worth and value they held. Many needed the beautiful reminders to be present not only to others, but to themselves. Many students needed to remember that they too are worthy and deserving of God's love and grace. This womanish mode of play of doing affirmations for one week let them embody God's love in new and necessary ways.

5. Statement written in an assignment and said in class by Olivia Haynes Ansari. Used with her kind permission.

FOUR

Twenty Questions:

Are We Doing Double

Dutch Yet?

Chapter 13
What Are the Questions?

In thinking about the double Dutch that a womanish pedagogy of play requires, it is important to ask the necessary questions. Asking the questions is not only playful but also offers information and critical awareness that can provide further understanding for critical consciousness. These questions are usually the who, what, why, and how of a sociocultural reality. Since a womanist consciousness and pedagogy are not the dominant narratives and have not traditionally been valued and lifted up, one must research and ask the questions in order to learn, grow, and gain understanding. Therefore, this section will ask the who, what, why, and how of a sociocultural reality for womanist scholars. Some of these answers were received from reading and research while others were done in the true womanist fashion of oral tradition through dialogue, conversation, during play, and at kitchen tables.[1] This was done in an attempt to highlight the experiences, understandings, work, and double Dutching that are involved in the implementation of a womanist pedagogy of play. While

1. Many of these conversations took place at the Religious Educators Association Meeting in St. Louis, MO, and the American Academy of Religion meeting in Boston, MA, in November of 2017. These conversations involved Black women who were tenured faculty, faculty on their way to tenure, newly hired faculty, doctoral students, and doctoral candidates. In an attempt to protect those who have requested anonymity, these answers will be based on actual experiences of the author, experiences and encounters that were witnessed, as well as anecdotes of other Black women, being used with permission. All identifying details have been obscured and the quotations are not verbatim, but summaries of experiences and encounters.

these experiences and understandings are specific for some Black women scholars, the need to understand and be critically aware of the systems that are in place that have not lifted up and continue to fail to uplift this kind of inclusive and holistic pedagogy should be called into question. As one gleans more information and becomes more aware and critically conscious of a womanist pedagogy of play for educating in faith, it is important to consider the following questions from a womanist perspective.

It is important to note two things before proceeding. The first is that none of what follows applies to every single Black woman. Black women and womanists are not monoliths and therefore everything that is said may be true for some, but not all Black women, womanists, students, or faculty. In fact, I feel it might be necessary to note that not all Black women identify as womanist either. The second important note is that, while women from all institutions were present, I will limit the responses here for only those Black women who do not teach or study in one of the 101 Historically Black Colleges or Universities in the United States. The latter would lead to different experiences and sets of answers to the questions below that are not within the scope of this book.

Who Womanists Teach

According to the US Department of Education and its National Center for Education Statistics, "in fall 2021, of the 1.5 million faculty at degree-granting postsecondary institutions, 56 percent were full time and 44 percent were part time. Faculty include professors, associate professors, assistant professors, instructors, lecturers, assisting professors, adjunct professors, and interim professors."[2] Among the 56 percent of full-time faculty only 6 percent identified as Black and

2. National Center for Education Statistics (2023). Characteristics of Postsecondary Faculty. *Condition of Education*. US Department of Education, Institute of Education Sciences. November 2023, from https://nces.ed.gov/programs/coe /indicator/csc. Table 315.20.

4 percent within that 6 percent were Black women. However, Black women are teaching to an undergraduate full- and part-time student body at public four-year institutions, which is 51 percent White (of the 15.4 million students, 7.8 million identify as White).[3] This often means that a portion of Black women are teaching to White students who do not look like them, share their culture, understand their embodied ways of knowing and being, or often know their history. In addition, at some institutions the Black woman professor may be the only Black faculty, the only woman faculty, or the only Black woman on faculty and thus students and faculty can find themselves challenged by the foreign Black woman's body itself. It creates a cultural shock or cognitive dissonance for some that is difficult to understand and teach or learn through. This cognitive dissonance along with White supremacy and much of what was discussed in part 1 of this book can come out in many forms. Some Black women professors have experienced extreme disrespect and disregard in the classroom because of our Black bodies, experiences, and teaching styles. Some students and other faculty repeatedly demand validation of our credentials to verify our intellectual capacity to teach. However, this same validation is not demanded of our White male or female colleagues.

A portion of Black women theological educators have also experienced backlash from some students and faculty for teaching and being ordained. Some students and faculty feel that women should not be in the pulpit or in the theological classroom. Black faculty, women faculty, and especially Black women faculty experience these realities at every staff meeting, walking across campus, in student meetings and interactions, and in every class we teach. This is the reality of being the 4 percent teaching to 51 percent.

---

3. National Center for Education Statistics (2022). Undergraduate Enrollment. *Condition of Education*. US Department of Education, Institute of Education Sciences. Retrieved June 16, 2023, from https://nces.ed.gov/programs/coe/indicator/cha. Table 306.10.

What Womanists Teach

In using womanist pedagogy it is imperative to double Dutch in order to teach the dominant narrative and the narrative of the marginalized as well. Womanists teach about the systems in place that have created such a dichotomy in order to call out injustice while also exposing students to other ideas, experiences, and realities. Womanists seek to cultivate character and enlarge one's capacity in the areas of scholarship, leadership, inclusion, creativity, and citizenship and therefore offer and teach a range of courses.[4] These courses seek to disrupt the dominant narrative while developing imagination, identity formation, intellectual rigor, and courage.

Womanists teach the curriculum while explaining and highlighting the hidden curriculum that undergirds it. Womanists not only teach the material but also the systems that have made this particular material superior, such as White supremacy, the need to decolonize, and have liberation theology. In doing this, womanists are not just teachers but political activists who seek to highlight, disrupt, decolonize, and deconstruct the systems of injustice that have placed one epistemology and narrative over another.

Why Womanists Teach

Womanists teach for many reasons. Among those reasons, for those who teach Christian education or theology, is to be a part of the transformation of people into disciples of Jesus and catalysts or agents of change and social transformation toward justice and liberation in the world. Womanists teach to empower, educate, and liberate. Womanists teach to help people understand the important link between praxis and theory. The link that helps one

---

4. Stacey Floyd-Thomas, "Cultivating a Pedagogy of Possibility: A Womanist Christian Social Ethicist's Teaching Philosophy." Teaching philosophy while associate professor of thics and director of Black church studies at Brite Divinity School in Fort Worth, TX.

understand "why people do what they do in order to figure out what ought to be done."[5]

Womanists teach to engage the person and their lived realities and experiences so that what they learn can be applicable for their life. Womanists seek to meet students where they are while offering hope for the future as students see that education goes beyond the classroom and lasts long after the classroom experience has taken place. Womanists teach because we often seek to bring social justice to the people who view justice as impossible and unattainable. Womanists teach because the world needs to hear and learn from another narrative. Womanists teach because we are doing the work our souls must have.[6]

How Womanists Teach

How womanists educate in faith is one of the most distinctive aspects about this work. In order for womanists to educate in faith we must do double Dutch. We must first learn how to jump the tightrope and then do the difficult work of incorporating a womanist rope at the same time.

Womanists can do this double Dutch to strategize in order to meet the demands of both "critical reflection and accountability whether it be personal, social, or institutional."[7] Womanists navigate both, affirming all of who students are and what they bring into the classroom space while also encouraging and raising questions about human existence, moral responsibility, freedom of choice, character, and conscientization.

To add an additional layer, womanists do all of this while being the 4 percent of African American faculty teaching to a 51 percent White student body. Womanists do this while being unapologetically who

5. Floyd-Thomas, "Cultivating a Pedagogy of Possibility."
6. This is a paraphrase of a quote attributed to the late Katie G. Cannon about call and vocation. See Floyd-Thomas, "Cultivating a Pedagogy of Possibility."
7. Floyd-Thomas, "Cultivating a Pedagogy of Possibility."

we are regardless of those telling us to be more White. We persist, regardless of students and faculty that continuously demand our credentials. We persist, regardless of those that objectify us and make us simply a Black female body. Womanists educate in faith from a place of experience and lived reality that is often foreign in the academy, using our engaged and embodied epistemologies and pedagogies, and yet we persist. And we don't only persist, we excel. We excel because of the Black women that have come before us. We excel because of the expansive and brilliant Black women we are. We excel because of the audacious Black women that are yet to come. We excel because we must . . . we must continue to tell another narrative and teach a pedagogy of love, embodiment, inclusion, excellence, hope, rage, pleasure, possibility, and liberation for all beings made in the image and likeness of God.

Chapter 14
What Is a Clearing Space?

What is a clearing space? I am sure many of us have heard about safe and brave spaces, but what is clearing space? "Clearing space" is a term that comes from Nobel Prize–winning American novelist Toni Morrison. In her work *Beloved*, she writes about "the Clearing." "The Clearing" is a space where people are able to laugh, dance, cry, be silent, sit, be together, mourn, grieve, celebrate, and most importantly be flesh.[1]

I prefer to use the term "clearing space," not only because it is the essence of Black women and womanism, but because wording like "safe" and "brave" does not get at the kind of environment this liberative work necessitates. I have often heard the usage of "safe space," which I am against using. Given the more recent reality of gun violence in schools, I feel it important to mention I am not talking about traditional physical safety from things like violence, but the idea of "safety" as a concept where people can share and be themselves because they are "safe" in the space. When I was a youth minister, I once had a young Black man tell me that safe space was bullshit. He continued to tell me that as a young Black man in the world there are places where he will never be safe and that I shouldn't promise him something that I couldn't deliver. This honest encounter shifted my entire perspective, because he was absolutely right. As educators we should never promise something we cannot deliver, especially something like safety. We "cannot promise that someone else will not say or do something offensive that destroys trust and leaves someone

1. Toni Morrison, *Beloved* (New York: Knopf, 1987), 101–4.

feeling belittled or devalued. To try to do so is counterproductive, dangerous and practically sets up the environment to fail as we are all human and will in fact mess up."[2] For many people of color there is no true safe space. There is no space where they will ever stop being a person of color or having their color seen. There is no such space where anyone can guarantee that someone will not say something ignorant or ask an offensive question. Hence, no space is ever truly safe and to pretend that this is not true is irresponsible and harmful.

I have come to see that even the usage of the word "safe" in this way is often a privilege, one that many bodies will never know or experience. If we cannot in fact provide "safety" for all bodies then we should not proclaim "safety" for any bodies. We should curate a space that is more honest and real in what it is and is not, what it can provide, and what our students need. This might take some co-creation, but I have often heard terms such as "brave space," "sacred space," "creative space," "challenging space," and it goes on. A few times students have chosen to name the space "safe space" but only after discussion and naming what can and cannot be provided in that space. The key here is communication and honesty about what is and is not possible in our particular classroom spaces.

When not referring specifically to womanish play, I sometimes utilize the phrase "brave space" in recognition that although one can never truly be safe, one can commit to being brave and vulnerable enough to take a risk to listen, support, disagree with, and challenge one another in life-giving ways that lead to challenging systems of oppression and personal and communal transformation. I use "brave space" as both an acknowledgment of the lack of fully safe spaces while also encouraging bravery and courage to still engage, share, and be present in the midst of difficult conversations. For me, brave space allows for creative tension and encourages debate and lively dialogue while demanding respect and honesty. This space also comes with the knowledge that everyone has made and will make mistakes

2. Lakisha Lockhart, "Enfleshing Catechesis through Embodied Space," in *Together Along the Way: Conversations Inspired by the Directory for Catechesis*, ed. Hosffman Ospino and Theresa O'Keefe (n.p.: Crossroad, 2021), 123.

and thus grace and mercy for one another are also necessary as long as they are accompanied by accountability and discussion. While I see the value in this term and will continue to use it, I feel that "clearing space" is more particular and specific to what is both necessary and curated when we engage womanish modes of play.

In thinking about my own classrooms when I engage womanish play, I often attempt to create a clearing space for my students. For me "clearing space is a space where people can come and dance, laugh, play, call each other in and out, let their hair down, embrace possibility and grace, lament and rage, and most importantly, be unapologetic and free. For me, this is the kind of space in which teaching and learning can thrive for all bodies."[3] I feel it important to mention that while I believe everyone can and should benefit and be liberated through womanish play and womanist clearing space, that does not mean that everyone can be a womanist. Let me be very clear here; to be a womanist is sacred, holy, and divine. It is reserved for those who live daily, breathe, suffer, rejoice, cry, shout, dance, and have their being within the flesh of a Black woman. For those that do not have their lived experience in this way, you can stand with, be an ally to, support, and practice the teachings of womanism while still respecting the sacredness of what it means to be a womanist.

Often when people think of play or possibly engaging in womanish modes of play, they think of fun and excitement. While it is true that play can engender fun and excitement, it also creates space for so much more. This space can hold the full range of our complex feelings and emotions. Play, much like the Divine, can hold our excitement and our disappointment, our joy and our rage, our peace and our frustration, our dance and our stillness, our healing and our hurt, our truth and our fear, our happiness and our sadness, our celebration and our lament; it holds our very flesh. Morrison speaks of the Clearing in her novel *Beloved*:

"Here," she said, "in this here place, we flesh; flesh that weeps, laughs; flesh that dances on bare feet in grass. Love it. Love it

3. Lockhart, "Enfleshing Catechesis through Embodied Space," 123.

hard. Yonder they do not love your flesh. They despise it. They don't love your eyes; they'd just as soon pick em out. No more do they love the skin on your back. Yonder they flay it. And O my people they do not love your hands. Those they only use, tie, bind, chop off and leave empty. Love your hands! Love them. Raise them up and kiss them. Touch others with them, pat them together, stroke them on your face 'cause they don't love that either. You got to love it, *you!*"[4]

Womanish modes of play invite the constant reminder of the importance of self. Not only of embracing self and engaging in community and culture, but also of embodying the very love of the Divine within one's very flesh. For Black women, the reminder to love our entire selves, including the flesh and bodies that have not always been our own, is vital and necessary. To have a space where you can both wrestle with and celebrate flesh is paramount. This is the kind of space that womanish modes of play inhabit and curate. It is more honest than safety and beyond being brave . . . it is real, transformative, revealing, creative, vulnerable, inviting, revelatory, and clearing. It is a sacred space for divine lives and fleshly bodies.

4. Morrison, *Beloved*, 103–4.

Chapter 15

Why Incorporate a Womanist Pedagogy of Play for Educating in Faith?

To make educating in faith a practice of freedom and transformation there must be an understanding of the teaching and pedagogical choices. In many ways, for education it all comes down to the mode and style of teaching that can make the difference—for freedom or for enslavement in the classroom. In trying to understand the style and pedagogical method I could easily describe the groundbreaking work around freedom of movement, observing with reverent love, and the importance of the teaching environment of Italian physician and educator Maria Montessori. This chapter could also easily lay out the foundational critical pedagogy that highlights the necessity of praxis and critical reflection as a primary way of knowing of Brazilian educator and philosopher Paulo Freire. Many, including myself and some of the Black women I will name, have been shaped by the work of both of these trailblazing religious educators, both of them steeped in their Christian faith. However, the work of bringing Black women's voices, experiences, and scholarship to the forefront, while not always easy, is one of the tasks that I have given myself in this work.

While honoring the foundational voices in religious education, I would like to move toward a womanist pedagogy of play of educating in faith. In order to do this, I must go back to the importance of history and heritage in the lives and experience of Black women. History shapes who we are, how we are seen in the world, and how we see/interpret ourselves. As an African American woman with a passion for religious education, I found it appalling that I could actually count the number of African American women religious educators that I knew. That did not even include the first Black woman in the United States to obtain a doctorate in religious education. Therefore, I knew that I needed to both learn and share about the history of African American women in religious education to move toward a true womanist approach to educating in faith. Moreover, as a womanist religious educator, I personally needed to honor and highlight the shoulders that I stand on and the women that have paved the way for me to even be writing this book.

Although there are more than three African American women religious educators, this chapter will focus on the work and pedagogy of Olivia Pearl Stokes, Anne Streaty Wimberly, and bell hooks and put them into conversation with Katie Geneva Cannon. I will begin by exploring the work of Olivia Pearl Stokes and her use of experience as a primary source of educating in faith. I will then discuss the work of Anne Streaty Wimberly highlighting her use of the story-linking model to educate in faith. I will then analyze the work of bell hooks and her understanding of education with attention to engagement through presence and community, looking specifically at her work in reconceptualizing knowledge, linking theory and practice, and incorporating passion and excitement. All such resources will contribute well to a womanist pedagogy. I will close this chapter by making connections with the work of these Black women educators and the work of explicitly womanist educator Katie G. Cannon in order to move toward a womanist pedagogy of play for educating in faith. My intent here is to highlight a particular method of teaching to create clearing spaces and support my claim that womanish modes of play can aid in both cognitive and affective well-being and in learning and educating in faith across difference.

Experiencing with Olivia Pearl Stokes

Olivia Pearl Stokes was born January 11, 1916, and grew up in Middlesex, North Carolina. Her family valued human dignity and education. Her life revolved around school and church where she became an ordained Baptist minister. She later became director of the Department of Education for the Massachusetts Council of Churches as well as holding other leadership roles in the area of church and religious education. She was so moved by the need for religious education and leadership in the church that she obtained a doctorate in religious education from the Columbia University Teachers College in New York in 1952, becoming the first Black woman in the United States to accomplish such a feat. She was affected by social events such as Jim Crow, civil rights, and the social and artistic center of Harlem. These events further cultivated her passion in religious education and specifically for the leadership training and development of young African Americans.

Stokes was deeply shaped by her experiences and discussions while traveling for work and leisure and she wanted to share and instill this in young African Americans through education and teaching. "This passion for teaching inspired her to explore a variety of teaching methods and techniques that would help persons to build relationships with others while increasing their knowledge."[1] "She believed that religious education should provide a variety of experiences and include a global focus."[2] With this global focus in mind, her pedagogy involved experience[3] and discussion from traveling, engaging with the Black church and Black community, and exposing students to African and African American heritage and culture.

Stokes was a huge proponent of traveling. She believed that traveling allowed for global and much-needed experiences and discussions that would then shape and mold a person. She stated that "travel is an effective mode of education . . . a wonderful way to learn about cultures and people."[4] She believed that when a person can see and

---

1. Y. Y. Smith and M. E. Moore, "Olivia Pearl Stokes: A Living Testimony of Faith," in *Faith of Our Foremothers: Women Changing Religious Education*, ed. B. Keely (Louisville: Westminster John Knox, 1997), 109.

2. Smith and Moore, "Olivia Pearl Stokes," 110.

3. It is important to note that Stokes's focus on experience was heavily influenced by John Dewey's work around experience and was highly praised at the Teacher's College at that time.

4. Smith and Moore, "Olivia Pearl Stokes," 110.

experience how another lives and makes meaning in the world they can begin to realize and become aware of their own morals and values and how they live them out. On one of her many trips to Ethiopia she noted a tradition that she witnessed in an Ethiopian church.

> When a child is blessed in the Ethiopian church, the father takes it to the altar, not the mother, and the mother is in a back room looking on . . . on the side all the fathers take the child to the altar. Today when we're in the midst of this liberated sexual behavior, which is neither love nor good sex, kids are having children and leaving the responsibility to mothers, sometimes to the grand-mothers. And it's really a tragic thing, and you would wish that the fathers were called to the altar by the mothers and the church, so that they would assume more responsibility. When people tell me, "that child doesn't have a father," I said, "every child had a father, maybe he's not responsible, but he's a parent."[5]

Here we see a prime example of how experiencing the culture of an-other brings about an assessment and analysis of one's own culture and way of doing things. Experiencing brings about consciousness and awareness. Stokes believed in the need to fully immerse one-self in cultures through experiences and reflection upon the expe-rience, and in conversation whenever possible. Discussion aided in this global focus as it encouraged further and more open dialogue with other cultures, genders, races, etc.[6] She often sought out these intercultural experiences and "gravitated toward international people who were different than all those around in the community where [she] lived" (Stokes interview, 48). She felt that these different experi-ences, discussions, and perspectives made her better and more aware not only of the other but of herself as well and she believed that all

5. Olivia Pearl Stokes, interview by Sandra Watson, Black Women Oral His-tory Project, September 25, 1979, Schlesinger Library, Radcliffe Institute, 39. Transcript and recording at https://hollisarchives.lib.harvard.edu/repositories /8/archival_objects/2485375. Hereafter, references to this source will appear in the text.

6. Smith and Moore, "Olivia Pearl Stokes," 109.

students and persons need these experiences and conversations to grow and learn.

As an African American ordained minister, Stokes also saw the necessity to engage the Black church in religious education. She felt folks needed to connect and be trained within the Black church since it was the center for the Black community.

> You see, the black church has always been three things to the black people, and this was true at Stokes Chapel. It was the center for all the social life, and launching all the talent in the congregation, membership, community and receiving people . . . it was, secondly, the center for the movement for freedom, for civic rights activity. So it was always there that we were political . . . the third thing the church was . . . it was the spiritual center you know, in a sense, the black church has been the psychiatrist for black people. They could come, and it was all right to give in to your feelings when you'd been hurt by the white man on the outside. (Stokes interview, 11)

She believed that religious education would have to engage and stem from the Black church as it was clearly the center of social life, activism, and civil rights, as well as the spiritual nexus of the Black community. The Black church was everything to the Black community and the religious education needed to come out of and flow back into the Black church in order to maintain and engage the Black community. She found engaging the Black community particularly important because she believed that American materialism was destroying their values and turning Black people into "rugged individualists and no longer the community of people, remembering that their heritage was out of Africa, or their heritage was out of the struggle to survive during the days of slavery" (Stokes interview, 31). So in order to engage the Black community she recognized that she had to go through the Black church.

In thinking of pedagogy, it is always crucial to be aware of context and community. Stokes was very aware of both as she not only engaged Black church leaders, but also provided a service that would highlight, teach, and expose students and congregants to African and African American heritage and culture. Honoring this desire for culture and world learning, Stokes advocated for Saturday Ethnic School, which was designed as a celebration of the values, art, and contributions of African and African American people (Stokes interview, 105). The offerings of the school would be as follows:

> Saturday Ethnic School would offer a curriculum centered on black history, black church history and contemporary issues viewed from the Black perspective. The school's major thrust would be to celebrate the genius of the Black experience, as expressed in the life of the individual, the Black family and the Black Christian community. It would aim to develop creativity within its members, to express their religious insights through drama, music, dance, painting, poetry and creative writing. (Stokes interview, 107)

Note well the emphasis on play as integral to the curriculum of the Saturday Ethnic School. This was how it would become a resource center for African culture and African American heritage for African Americans. This would be a space where Black people could learn about their history, culture, and themselves. It would promote self-awareness, self-development, and critical consciousness within the Black community that was often lacking in religious education.

Stokes believed that pedagogy should broaden the horizons and introduce individuals to new cultures. Stokes affirmed that education "is a holistic process, involving the entire person . . . experience was essential to the learning process, and she encouraged people to share with one another and to experience others' worlds. In her view, people need to experience the world because education is more than an intellectual exercise" (Stokes interview, 114). Using Stokes's pedagogy of highlighting experience and discussion through travel, engagement with the Black church and the Black community, and highlighting African and African American culture and heritage through Saturday Ethnic School, educating in faith becomes a liberating act. This liberating education can begin to "transform structures so that persons become beings for themselves, not instruments manageable by others and by structures to which they have to conform."[7] It acknowledges that Black people, while often oppressed, are also persons made in the image and likeness of God and deserving of dignity, worth, and religious education that also speaks to their experience, heritage, and culture. This liberating religious education allows persons of all races and ethnicities to become more aware not only of the importance of Black heritage and culture but of other cultures as well. "The world that we're living in, and the world that young people are going to be living in, is going to be multi-cultured, multi-ethnic, and multi-ideological. We've got to have all these ideologies understood, appreciated, respected—pluralism is the word" (Stokes interview, 62–63). According to Stokes some of the ways to prepare and make space for this multicultural, multiethnic, and ecumenical world is through traveling in order to experience and reflect upon culture and rituals in order to gain consciousness and become more aware of one's own culture, values, and morals. Another way is through involving the Black church in order to engage the Black community—as a community—to give them opportunities to learn, explore, and be exposed to their own history and heritage along with that of those who are different from them as well.

Story-Linking with Anne Streaty Wimberly

Anne Streaty Wimberly was born in Anderson, Indiana, on June 10, 1936. Her father was a minister in the Methodist church for thirty years and her mother was a homemaker. Growing up her church worked hard to stand in the gap for the children through helping and equipping them for the future. This preparation included aiding youth like Wimberly to cultivate and nurture their gifts. This inspired her to nurture gifts in other Black youth as the executive

---

7. Olivia Pearl Stokes, "Education in the Black Church: Design for Change," in *Who Are We? The Quest for a Religious Education*, ed. John H. Westerhoff (Birmingham: Religious Education, 1978), 231.

director of the Youth Hope-Builders academy at the Interdenominational Theological Center in Atlanta, Georgia, where she is currently their professor emerita of Christian education.

Wimberly was shaped by the nurturing and story sharing that occurred in her childhood, and she has carried this with her into her teaching. The core of her pedagogy to educate in faith is through story-linking. Story-linking is a narrative-based process that invites participants to connect the stories of their lives with the stories of their ancestors in Christian faith and the stories of the Scriptures.[8] Wimberly states it more thoroughly:

> Participants link with Bible stories/texts by using them as a mirror through which they reflect critically on the liberation and vocation they are seeking or have already found. The purpose of this linkage is to help persons be aware of the liberating activity of God and God's call to vocation—living in the image of Jesus Christ—in both biblical and present times. (Wimberly, xi)

This model aids in clarifying vocation and discernment as well as opening a space for individuals to use the Bible stories as mirrors to critically reflect on their own lives, where they have already been liberated and where they need wisdom and guidance for ongoing liberation. It allows for individuals to "recover the central role of story and storytelling for the liberating wisdom and hope-building vocation" (Wimberly, 4). This process of story-linking involves four phases: "(1) engaging everyday story, (2) engaging the Christian faith story in the Bible, (3) engaging Christian faith stories from the African American heritage, and (4) engaging in Christian ethical decision making" (Wimberly, 26).

Phase one of the story-linking process is engaging people's everyday story. In this phase persons use their personal stories as a lens to look through as one focuses on various aspects of Christian edu-

8. Anne Streaty Wimberly, *Soul Stories: African American Christian Education* (Nashville: Abingdon, 2005), xi. Hereafter, references to this source will appear in the text.

cation. Here "the intent is to acknowledge that Christian education leaders/teachers and participants already have an agenda when they come to Christian education. Our stories are the agenda we bring to our study of the Christian faith story in the Bible and our Christian faith heritage" (Wimberly, 27). Everyone has a story and it is important to know that everyone colors their learning with their own personal stories and experiences. Each person brings their stories, their personal and cultural identities, social contexts, interpersonal relationships, life events, and life meanings with them to encounter God's word through Scripture or the faith stories of their ancestors. As religious educators, we must remember that not only do educators bring all of this, but so do each of our students. It is the educator's responsibility to enable and curate space for students to feel welcome and open to share their own stories and draw them out into their larger community if they choose to share. An important thing to note is that no one, no student and no faculty member, owes anyone their story. There should always be a choice and not a mandate as our stories are our own and we choose when and how to share them—always.

Phase two of the process is engaging the Christian faith story in the Bible. In this phase the personal stories or the case studies that were shared are linked with "the Story of God and the good news of Jesus Christ found in Scripture" (Wimberly, 30). This phase requires preparation by the religious educator. The Scripture passage that is going to be used should "already be provided as printed lesson material" in order to "engage the Scripture in the story-linking process" (Wimberly, 30). The hope in the preparation is that "the Scripture is chosen specifically because it addresses concretely the nature of God's action and provides wisdom the African American Christian seeks in her or his quest for liberation and hope-filled vocation" (Wimberly, 31). This gives participants "direct access" to the Scripture Story rather than what is mediated or interpreted by the educator or minister. Further, it deeply engages people's own lives with the biblical stories, encouraging them to personally encounter God's word for their lives.

Phase three of the process is engaging Christian faith stories from African American heritage. This phase is designed to link the faith heritage of African American Christians with the everyday personal life stories. "These stories will include not only stories of African American heroes and heroines well known to most African Americans but also stories of family heroes and heroines . . . which bring added meaning and depth to the story-linking process" (Wimberly, 31). This is extremely important for African Americans as it involves learning about African American history and stories of African Americans that can inspire younger African Americans. It draws upon both tradition and Scripture.

The fourth and last phase of the story-linking process is engaging in Christian ethical decision making. This phase is designed to aid persons in investigating liberating options for wise and "hope-building" outcomes (Wimberly, 33). It is in this phase that "persons bring to bear on their life stories ideas, wise insights, and discernment from the first three phases of the story-linking process" (Wimberly, 33). It is also in this phase that persons hopefully move toward claiming the Story of God as their own and become more responsible and energized in working to realize both personal and social liberation. The whole pedagogy, hopefully, is to result in concrete "liberating and vocational actions" (Wimberly, 33).

It is important to note that for this process to take place the educator must "create a nurturing space for story-sharing and compassionate listening" (Wimberly, 35). By creating an atmosphere of compassion and openness, people will feel welcome to share and build trust.

Engaging with bell hooks

Gloria Jean Watkins, who is better known by her pen name bell hooks, was born September 25, 1952, in Hopkinsville, Kentucky. She was educated in both racially segregated and integrated schools. However, she found learning in an integrated school very difficult and sought to change that as an educator. She was influenced by the work of Toni Morrison, who was the focus of her dissertation. Her work lies in the intersections of race, gender, oppression, and class issues. Her work in education is greatly influenced by Paulo Freire. In her work, she explores ways in which the classroom can become a source of liberation, as opposed to the oppressive hierarchical systemic power authority that it typically is. She advocates for a more engaged pedagogy that involves presence, community, and passion. This engaged pedagogy becomes a practice of freedom when one teaches in such a way that "anyone can learn."[9] In order to do this one must reconceptualize knowledge and how one knows, link theory and practice, empower students, encourage dialogue, and engage in multicultural education to make teaching and learning boundary crossing and transgressive. She believes that critical consciousness and thinking are essential for one's epistemology.[10] By critical consciousness she means that persons must become aware of their own situatedness in the world and begin to reflect and act accordingly. When these ideas, concepts, structures, and one's situatedness within the world have all been critically reflected upon and have become practice, education can become a practice of freedom. The classroom can become a space where students and teachers are able to be honest, build community, dismantle hierarchical systems that seek to oppress and under-represent minority cultures. By this kind of theory and practice pedagogy, learning and teaching can be liberating.

In exploring hooks's engaged pedagogy, I understand engagement through presence and community with passion and excitement not only as a way of knowing, but as a way of reconceptualizing knowledge altogether. Classrooms are places where hierarchy and power are manifested in ways that hooks wants to dismantle with her engaged pedagogy. In order to combat this power that permeates the classroom "through conceptualization of knowledge and the manner of transmission,"[11] hooks seeks to reconceptualize knowledge through her

9. hooks, *Teaching to Transgress: Education as the Practice of Freedom* (New York: Routledge, 1994), 13.

10. Here hooks is influenced by Paulo Freire's understanding of praxis as a primary way of knowing through action, critical consciousness, and dialogue.

11. Florence Namulundah, *bell hooks' Engaged Pedagogy: A Transgressive Education for Critical Consciousness* (London: Bergin & Garvey, 1998), 95. Hereafter, references to this source will appear in the text.

pedagogy, which aims to "transgress conventional educational norms and practices, and to create strategies for making the teaching/learning process more dynamic, exciting, and meaningful to students" (Namulundah, 100). These practices include re-evaluating curriculum and looking to the body as a way of knowing. She believes that the curriculum should "interrogate White supremacist, patriarchal, capitalist ideologies reflected in the notion of standardized curriculum, pedagogical orientations, and a static view of social reality" (Namulundah, 99). This can be changed by encouraging critical consciousness[12] among students and educators, recognizing more cultural diversity, and reflecting this diversity within the curriculum, which includes the addition of feminist, womanist, and other emancipatory voices.

Another key component in reconceptualizing knowledge is looking at the wisdom of the body and allowing space for touch and movement in the classroom. "To make a place for touch in the classroom is to resist the closing of our ways of knowing that take us beyond words and demand we listen to the body and know ourselves as flesh."[13] While touch is quite powerful, it is also important to note that in this day and age there should be guidelines for this so that it does not invade privacy, become exploitative, or move to a place of sexual misconduct. As a Black woman, hooks recalls the history of the experience of suffering for Black people and the knowledge that was gained through the body. She affirms that "it is a way of knowing that is often expressed through the body, what it knows, what has been deeply inscribed on it through experience. This complexity of experience can rarely be voiced and named from a distance."[14] Education praises intellectual knowledge over bodily wisdom, but here hooks brings the body back to the educational space and allows it to take its place as a way of knowing in the world.

12. There must be acknowledgment that this phrase and hooks's understanding of it come from Brazilian educator Paulo Freire.

13. bell hooks, *Teaching Critical Thinking: Practical Wisdom* (New York: Routledge, 2010), 157.

14. hooks, *Teaching to Transgress*, 91.

In diversifying and changing the concept of knowledge, hooks understands the importance of linking the practice to a foundational theory. For hooks "theory provides venue for analyzing experience (practice)" (Namulundah, 102). As an educator who values cultural studies, hooks finds linking theory and practice necessary in creating new space. She affirms that "cultural studies must combine theory and practice in order to affirm and demonstrate pedagogical practices engaged in creating a new language, rupturing disciplinary boundaries, decentering authority, and rewriting the institutional and discursive borderlands . . . for reasserting the relationship between agency, power, and struggle."[15] It is only when the practice links with theory that new space can be made for important issues, such as multiculturalism, interculturalism, and teaching and learning across difference.

Making space for cultural pluralism not only empowers students who are marginalized but also "helps develop collaboration and solidarity among students in school" (Namulundah, 119). Multicultural education does more than just incorporate various cultures within class syllabi; it "addresses issues of cultural alienation, resistance to school learning, and subsequently low academic performance in minority students" (Namulundah, 86). It takes critical consciousness on the part of educators to realize and become aware of ourselves and our classroom's situatedness within this system. Critical thinking and practice about multicultural education forces educators and institutions to be aware of how these issues of alienation, being under-represented in school, and feeling powerless affect and shape various interactions or lack of interactions in the classroom (Namulundah, 119). This involves a great deal of risk and vulnerability that not only demands critical consciousness but also incites critical consciousness in students (Namulundah, 122). When educators are able "to incorporate other voices and acknowledge each student's presence and to integrate subordinated cultural histories," then multicultural education is happening and the classroom becomes a more welcoming and holistic place that invites honesty and

15. hooks, *Teaching to Transgress*, 129.

openness (Namulundah, 122). When students feel welcome and heard, they become empowered.

Student empowerment relies on the student-teacher relationship, safe space,[16] and classroom community.[17] As hooks affirms, the relationship between the student and the teacher must be one of mutuality (Namulundah, 83) that aids in creating learning communities that "avoid the trap of coercive hierarchies in empowering and respecting the contribution of both students and teachers while honoring individual differences" (Namulundah, 106). In honoring each student's presence, voice, and lived experience, this engaged pedagogy goes "beyond the mere sharing of information to a more holistic involvement with students" (Namulundah, 114). This honoring and valuing of students' presence builds community through "creating a sense that there is shared commitment and a common good that binds us."[18] This type of experience brings about solidarity and a beloved community that allows for the educator to embrace, incorporate, and share their passion and excitement with the community that has been created.

When educators are able to dismantle the compartmentalization that is promoted by this mind/body split in education we are able to "recover ourselves, our feelings, our passion" (Namulundah, 126), both inside and outside the classroom. This sharing of our passion and excitement makes the classroom a more dynamic, energetic, fun place where transformation and change become possible (Namulundah, 125). I would add play into this area as it is essential in building learning communities and in sharing and receiving stories that "open our minds and hearts."[19] Adding play and our passion and excitement is a way of linking theory to practice to the religious educational experience that not only honors the cognitive but also the affective ways of knowing

16. hooks, *Teaching to Transgress*, 39.
17. As a reminder, the term "safe space" here is a term that hooks uses and one that I do not use or agree with using. I prefer "brave space" or "clearing space."
18. hooks, *Teaching to Transgress*, 40.
19. hooks, *Teaching Critical Thinking*, 51–52.

that are essential for a more holistic education—so demanded by the very nature of Christian faith.

While there are many others I could have utilized in this chapter, I focus on these three Black women because their models and ideas of story-linking, community, mutuality, excitement, travel, experience, and disrupting oppressive and unjust systems coincide with my idea of womanism and a womanist pedagogy of play.

In moving toward a womanist pedagogy of play for educating in faith, one must take the history and heritage of Olivia Pearl Stokes's use of experience, along with Anne Streaty Wimberly's story-linking model, and bell hooks's engaged pedagogy to heart. The experiences and methods of these Black women, and the other Black women who are not named explicitly in this work, must be considered. The work of these Black women must be considered because a womanist pedagogy must emerge from and be empowered by the actual experiences and understandings of Black women. While the hope is that a womanist pedagogy of play will aid in learning and teaching for persons of all races, ethnicities, genders, etc., what makes a womanist pedagogy of play womanist is that it emerges distinctly from the experience of struggle, oppression, and survival of Black women. Since it does emerge from the real-life experiences of survival of Black women it has a way of challenging and deconstructing conventional, oppressive, and patriarchal theologies, ideologies, and systems that are in place and in turn offers up more holistic, engaged, embodied, and inclusive educational methods and practices—especially for educating in faith.[20]

Womanist educator and ethicist Katie Cannon describes womanist pedagogy as

the process by which we bring this kind of knowing about African American women into relation with a justice-praxis for members of our species and the wider environment in which we are

20. Katie Geneva Cannon, *Katie's Canon: Womanism and the Soul of the Black Community* (New York: Continuum, 1995), 137. Hereafter, references to this source will appear in the text.

> situated in order to resist conditions that thwart life, arriving at
> new understandings of our doing, knowing, and being. . . . Our
> womanist work is to draw on the rugged endurance of Black folks
> in America who outwit, outmaneuver, and outscheme social sys-
> tems and structures that maim and stifle mental, emotional, and
> spiritual growth. (Cannon, 135, 141)

In other words, not only does a womanist pedagogy need to emerge
from a Black woman's experience, but it must also make space for
the various ways in which Black women come to know, to be, and to
take part in making meaning and living in the world—their cultural
reality. This must involve disrupting oppressive systems that do not
make space for the creative and embodied realities of not just Black
women but all people. In order to do this effectively Cannon offers
two methods. The first method is metalogues, or what Cannon refers to as "concentric circles,"[21] and the second is doing the "dance of
redemption."[22] Both methods must go hand in hand, just as doing
double Dutch requires both ropes to turn at the same time. While
this provides another level of difficulty it is necessary and is meant
to be disruptive, yet liberating work.

The first method of metalogues/concentric circles involves the
interconnecting of disciplines. As Cannon defines it, metalogues are
"highly organized or specialized forms of logic, designating new but
related disciplines that can deal critically with the nature, structure,
or behavior of the original discourse, talk, performance, or recital"
(Cannon, 136). In other words, these metalogues are ways of thinking
that critically analyze not only a problematic issue or behavior, but the
structures and systems in place that have allowed, made space for, and/
or encouraged the problematic issue or behavior. So in order to talk

21. See Cannon, *Katie's Canon*, 191. Concentric circles have a common center.
Picture a bullseye or target in which there is a center and circles that extend and
circle outward.

22. Katie Cannon adapted feminist ethicist Beverly Wildung Harrison's
"dance of redemption." This model describes the process of recognizing oppression and forming ethical decisions and moral stances in relation to it. See Cannon, *Katie's Canon*, 163–64.

effectively about a womanist pedagogy of play there must be concentric circles of discourse which reflect not only on the problem but the systems that created it and allowed the problem to persist, as well in order to effectively provide inclusive and disruptive womanist work.

The first wheel in the concentric circles is much like that of the tightrope. It is one filled with traditional European male thinking, language, knowing, and understanding. It is this wheel "whose very language of objective universality masks our existence, forces us to persist in binary oppositions, and looks at Black women as superfluous appendages, saddled with odd concerns about race, sex, and class oppression" (Cannon, 138). This is by far the biggest and most well-known wheel and the one that must be addressed and have its oppressive and unjust systems and beliefs disrupted. This is along the lines of the work that bell hooks seeks to do in her engaged pedagogy. Within this first wheel is a second wheel that specifically addresses the culture, history, beliefs, and experiences of Afro-Christians and members of the Black church community (Cannon, 138). This is where oral histories, stories, and cultures are passed down among generations to continue the lineage that the dominant European discourse often fails to mention. This would incorporate the story-linking of Anne Streaty Wimberly and the experience through traveling of Olivia Pearl Stokes.

The third and smallest wheel inside both of these wheels that must be lifted up in order to have a true womanist pedagogy of play is the wheel of Black women's experiences, texts, oral histories, and interpretations. This would involve engaging Black women authors, poets, artists, choreographers, etc. Any pedagogy that seeks to engage a womanist consciousness must begin with the larger circle, but always with a hermeneutics of suspicion and a desire for disruption as it moves inward.

While cultivating a pedagogy that uses the concentric circles one must also do the dance of redemption (Cannon, 140). This dance involves the acknowledgment of oppression and injustice and the formulation of moral and ethical decisions in response to that acknowledgment. This dance is a free style dance with no particular entry point or choreography to follow, just dancing as one acknowledges, discovers, and responds. The parts of the dance are: conscientization, emancipatory historiography, theological resources, norms clarification, strategic options, annunciation and celebration, and re-reflection/strategic action (Cannon, 140).

Conscientization involves the kind of critical social and historical analysis of causes and consequences throughout history that lead to the realization that what is normative and what is reality are not always synonymous. This can even lead to cognitive dissonance when realizing that the two do not match up because of various oppressions or injustices. Emancipatory historiography is the critical awareness and reflection upon one's social cultural history with the fantastic hegemonic imagination and the systems that hold various structures of oppression and injustice in place. Theological resources require critical awareness and reflection upon one's theological disciplines and spiritual community and the ways in which these theological resources liberate or hold on to various structures of oppression. Norm clarifications involve critical awareness and asking questions in reference to values, accountability, and one's stance in light of the awareness of various systems of oppression and injustice in the world and in one's community. Strategic options are when one begins to act upon one's critical awareness and reflection by asking how one can utilize one's new knowledge and what might the consequences be for utilizing or not utilizing that knowledge to aid in liberating or upholding oppressive structures. Annunciation and celebration are the realization that all persons are relational beings who cannot do this work by themselves alone. We must remember that together all persons can celebrate, lament, challenge and turn surviving into thriving. Re-reflection/strategic action is the beginning of this dance again with new insights gained from critical reflection and awareness of new oppressive and unjust systems that are not liberative for everyone.

This dance involves critical thinking and reflection on every aspect of life from the personal to the institutional, as well as the historical, and looking at the various systems in place that are oppressive. As one begins to understand these new systemic, historic, and personal realizations, this dance continues through reflection, learning, and growing as it turns into double Dutch that can enkindle the world.

Chapter 16

Womanish Modes of Play

Enkindle the World

Here I offer the final part of the womanist definition and the accompanying ethical tenet of womanism from Alice Walker and Stacey Floyd-Thomas.

> Womanist is to feminist as purple is to lavender.[1]

> The fourth tenet of womanist ethics obliges black women to critically engage their world at the intersections of their oppressions since they have borne the brunt of social injustice throughout the history of the modern world. As a result, they have an unshakable belief that their survival strategies must entail more than what others have provided as an alternative. . . . Womanist ethics mandates that for black women, true liberation necessitates no compromise, mortgage, or trade-off. What it means to be a black woman in this regard is to struggle ceaselessly to the fullest extent in search of freedom, justice, and equality.[2]

Here there is a focus on actively engaging at the intersections of oppression and injustice, what I name in this book as enkindling the world. In order to dismantle the various systems of oppression and injustice one must set fire to the world through a critical social con-

---

1. Alice Walker, *In Search of Our Mothers' Gardens: Womanist Prose* (New York: Harcourt, Brace, 1983), xi–xii.
2. Stacey Floyd-Thomas, *Mining the Motherlode: Methods in Womanist Ethics* (Cleveland: Pilgrim, 2006), 10–11.

sciousness that encourages emancipatory activism, legislation, and advocacy. There are many ways in which to be catalysts of change and transformation in the world; womanism lifts up this kind of critical engagement with the world. Black women were, and in many spaces still are, oppressed and treated unjustly. This part of the definition resists that reality by calling people to be catalysts of change and actively seeking out ways to disrupt these systems of oppression and injustice. This looks different for each person, depending on their own gifts and talents. And when a community of people can come together to resist injustice, their voices and potential to effect change are stronger.

This part is not easy, but it is necessary. As mentioned previously, God wants us all to be free; one cannot embrace one's self, embody God's love, engage in one's culture and community, and yet still allow others to be dehumanized and pushed to the margins of society. This would be against what God desires for God's people. Part of what it means to be a womanist is to be brave enough to challenge the corrupt system, and to support, encourage, and stand with others who are doing the same. It means resisting by asking conscious questions, remembering critically, creatively, and collaboratively imagining and living into emancipatory hope.

This kind of setting fire to the world takes honesty and courage, and it is hopefully contagious. *This kind* of thinking and action in the classroom and in the church reminds participants that the world does not begin and end in the classroom or the church, but extends into the world. It reminds participants, educators, and ministers alike that, as a person of faith, one is called to stand up to injustice and oppression wherever they live and breathe. *This kind* of thinking and action builds a classroom that can have fun, be creative, spontaneous, and imaginative while setting fire to the world together by disrupting it and then transforming it.

To aid in creating *this kind* of active classroom, the educator can offer womanish modes of play that promote engagement and participation in dismantling distorted systems. These womanish modes of play can be, but are not limited to, doing an obstacle course, bearing witness to graffiti art, creating, and protesting. These practices can ignite a sense of communal and civic responsibility, care for self, and care for those who are oppressed.

Essentials and Suggestions

This mode of play invites participants to actively work together for a common goal of challenging and pushing back against a form of oppression or injustice. Having participants reflect on how Jesus resisted and pushed back against injustice and oppression in the biblical texts will aid participants in understanding the need for and importance of this work. Participants must come together to reflect on Scripture, talk about what the injustices are, think about their own gifts and talents and how they can be used to meet a need, combat an injustice, and then tangibly do so individually and together. This will take time, negotiation, creativity, and imagination. It will build a classroom bond as well as aid in engendering creative critical thinkers and activists that are creatively transforming the world for the better.

Womanish Modes of Play: Enkindle the World

- *Womanish mode of play:* Obstacle course.
- *Materials needed:* Use items that you would like to create an obstacle course. Things such as jump ropes, hula hoops, chairs, bubbles, blindfolds, big bouncy balls, small tennis balls, etc. (you can make an obstacle course out of almost anything you already have—be creative!).
- *Environment/space:* Open space where students can engage together without risk of getting hurt.
- *Directions:* After discussing the importance of enkindling the world, invite your students to participate in an obstacle course. It would be helpful if you already had it set up or you could invite your students to help you set it up. Be sure to make it the appropriate level of challenge for your students. Curate space for them to play and

think about the many obstacles in their lives and the world and how they might enkindle it.

- *Questions for reflection:*
  - Did you have fun?
  - What was the hardest part? The most fun?
  - How did you feel about doing this with a partner or team?
  - What is sticking with you?
  - If you could do it again, what would you do differently?
  - How might you use this as a metaphor for how you engage in obstacles in life?

- *Womanish mode of play:* Witnessing mural/graffiti art.
- *Materials needed:* Mural/graffiti art to witness and time to spend with it.
- *Environment/space:* Space to witness the mural/graffiti art wherever it appears.
- *Directions:* After discussing the importance of enkindling the world, invite your students to participate in a mural/graffiti tour of your town. If this isn't possible, invite them to look online for a mural/graffiti art that speaks to them. Invite them to take time and really witness what is depicted in the artwork and think about how it might be enkindling the world.
- *Questions for reflection:*
  - What did you witness?
  - Where is the piece located and why might this be important?
  - What moved you about it?
  - What do you think led to the artist creating that piece in that place?
  - Why do you think this piece of art matters?
  - What is sticking with you?

- *Womanish mode of play:* Create to enkindle.
- *Materials needed:* Materials that are needed are dependent upon what students are wanting to create. If doing this in class you might want to have several different items such as posters and markers,

items for quilting by hand, paint and brushes, clay, scissors and glue, and paper and pencils.

- *Environment/space:* Space to create.
- *Directions:* After discussing the importance of enkindling the world, invite your students to create something that speaks to the systems of oppression and injustice that they experience or witness in their context. (e.g., quilting, graffiti, photo collage, piece of artwork, song, poetry, public statement, etc.). Invite them to enkindle the world with what they create.
- *Questions for reflection:*
  - How did it feel to create something with your hands?
  - What did you create and why?
  - What will you do with it?
  - How are you enkindling the world with this piece?
  - What is sticking with you?

- *Womanish mode of play:* Protesting.
- *Materials needed:* Posters, markers, water, and various other items or materials.
- *Environment/space:* Space to create signs or desired items and whatever space might be used for the protest.
- *Directions:* After discussing the importance of enkindling the world, invite your students to participate in a protest that they feel passionate about. If this isn't possible, invite them to take part in a mock protest in class on a past issue that they found important and are passionate about. Reminding them to always consider their safety, offer them the opportunity to get involved as they feel comfortable. Maybe they are comfortable creating the signs or maybe they prefer to be outside in the midst holding up that sign. There is room and space for all to participate at their level of comfort, including active witnessing. Curate space for students to enkindle the world through protesting.
- *Questions for reflection:*
  - What did you choose to protest? Why?
  - What difference do you think your protesting brought about?

- What did you enkindle?
- How did it feel to participate in a protest?
- What is sticking with you?

Practical Example of Enkindle the World

In thinking about enkindling the world you could invite your students to create something that actively and creatively addresses a particular injustice in their context or the world. You could read and reflect on Matthew 21:12-17—when Jesus cleansed the temple and turned over tables—and discuss God's desire for liberation for all people. Students could then discuss how they would creatively address something that could tear down a current oppressive system.

When I did this in one of my classes, one student wrote a poem about the different realities of a particular part of town, another made a plan to encourage and aid in voting, while another noticed that of all the various bus stops along a particular bus route, only one had a covering. Noticing the covering was in a particularly affluent area, adjacent to a seminary, he began his campaign to get coverings on the other bus stops that were not in affluent areas. Another student continued her work aiding and supporting young Black girls and children with mentoring and education.

I will note that while I asked for individual creations, this can also be done in small groups or as one big group. I imagine that one group might choose to create a garden where the participants grow vegetables and herbs in order to teach people about sustainable living and to give others food that is not drenched in pesticides and chemicals. Another group might decide to create a quilt or a mural addressing a particular issue or injustice. A different group might decide to invite the entire school to pray for a particular injustice by making a photograph prayer wall where people can place photos of what they would like to pray for, and have a specific time to come and pray at the wall each day or each week. In one of my classes one of the groups created a beautiful board game called Cannonopoly (named for Katie G. Cannon) to introduce people to womanism and the womanist tenets. It was one of the most brilliant manifestations of a womanist pedagogy of play that I have seen. I am on a mission to turn this into an actual game that can be purchased and played, so feel free to look it up and purchase it once it is available.

The hope is that in creating and critically engaging together in things happening in the world more people can become conscious of corrupt and oppressive systems. In realizing the Christian mandate and example in Jesus Christ to resist injustice and strive for the liberation of all people, students will work together to become catalysts enkindling the world with their creativity, imagination, prayers, and bodies in "this here flesh."[3] This work of enkindling the world and setting things ablaze is what leads to change and brings about flourishing and freedom of all people made in the image and likeness of God.

3. Toni Morrison, *Beloved* (New York: Knopf, 1987), 103.

Conclusion

As a religious educator and practical theologian, I must conclude this book by offering the benefits of this work and considering how to train and prepare theological educators to engage in these practices in the classroom. I will address the value, not only for Black women, but for all persons. By utilizing womanish modes of play as pedagogical tools, one can engage and educate the whole person in transformative and liberating ways. Therefore, not only Black women, but everyone can begin to tell a new narrative, one in which their playful identities are known and embraced. A new narrative in which womanish modes of play not only provide access to the Christian story but curate clearing spaces for one's own story and welcome the opportunity to re-story. A new narrative that invites persons to become more critically conscious, allowing for meaning making and the cognitive and affective well-being of persons with bodies that are connected to and liberated by and with Jesus Christ.

So What?

It is a fact that jumping rope is easier than doing double Dutch. One can jump rope by oneself, and there is only one rope involved. While it still requires a sense of rhythm and an understanding of centrifugal force, it is still focused on that one main and only rope. Double Dutch is more difficult as another rope is added. This requires even more focus and accounting for the centrifugal force of two ropes. It requires more work, but more is to be gained in learning, stamina, balance, and focus. This book is inviting us to do the more difficult task of double Dutching together. In combining this tightrope with a womanist rope one can begin to engage in more inclusive, intersectional, transformative, and life-giving work for all persons involved. To do this requires doing the hard work of becoming critically conscious and aware that there are other narratives than just the dominant one that is prostituted as *the* truth. The beauty of doing double Dutch is that it makes space not just for the narrative of Black women, but for everyone . . . including you.

Many Black women have experienced the effects and consequences of living in a country where the fantastic hegemonic imagination runs rampant. Turning the tightrope and the womanist ropes together involves understanding and appreciating the narratives of others, which cannot be done until we curate clearing space to listen, see, and begin to value the intersectional identities, ways of being, ways of knowing, ways of making meaning, and ways of communicating of all people. This kind of work enriches everyone when we learn from and with, instead of fear or ignore, the other. We begin to see the strength in difference and diversity that allows us to be our embodied true selves and make clearing space for the other to be their embodied true self.

While this work is written from a womanist consciousness, experience, voice, and theological anthropology it makes room for all voices, experiences, and narratives—as long as they are open to such learning and changing that leads to liberation. That is what makes womanism so uniquely fitting as the additional rope in double Dutch—because womanists' experience and culture has provided Black women with a deep empirical knowledge and understanding of exclusion, oppression, and injustice on multiple levels. Which is why womanists can not only believe in but push for inclusion and the valuing of intersectional identities and ways of knowing and being for the flourishing of all persons.

Why?

While acknowledging a larger history and narrative, womanish modes of play also resist this narrative that was created from the dominant group in power to only reflect what they deemed as right. This meant the narrative of native persons, enslaved persons, same gender-loving persons, trans persons, disabled/differently abled persons, and other oppressed and marginalized persons and groups were not valued or heard. Womanish modes of play make space for the oppressed and marginalized voices, narratives, and experiences as they encourage persons to care for what is different. These embodied practices inform everyone that there is more than just one narrative, one body, one gender, and one racial group that is important and valuable. These womanish playful practices form persons in the knowledge that all persons are beings of dignity and value with bodies and stories that need to be told in the world, especially in the classroom. These practices can transform the traditional and oppressive ways of knowing and doing things into more inclusive, expansive, fun, and life-giving ways of knowing and being in the world.

There needs to be a deconstruction of the dominant oppressive structure within educational institutions for transformative learning to happen. I believe womanish modes of play can aid in the disruption and hopeful deconstruction of the power and hierarchical structures within theological educational classrooms. Incorporating critical consciousness into classrooms encourages persons to come to know for themselves and begin to see their own situatedness in the world. This leads to persons working to eradicate oppression and systems of power that are in universities and religious institutions. Womanish modes of play invite both the educator and the students to challenge the dominant narrative and to think critically, to reflect, and act using both their minds *and* their bodies. It invites both students and teachers to see each other and to notice where oneself and the other are not seen in the world and to begin to rectify it.

One way in which educators can rethink ways of knowing, being, and expressing oneself to transform the classroom and the church into more liberating and holistic places is through engaging the body in the learning process. The classroom must not solely be about the teacher but about the voices, expressions, stories, and experiences of the student as well. Fun, excitement, and spontaneity are characteristics of play that can not only add to the classroom experience but also disrupt the various systems of oppression and offer something more holistic in its place. Through engaging the body in the learning process, difference is recognized and respected in each person and room is made for the diversity in expressions and experiences. Embodied teaching, learning, and practices, such as womanish modes of play, provide clearing space for students and teachers—clearing and ontological space for individuals to be exactly who they are and to encounter God through their preferred medium.

It is through playful womanish practices that we begin to see each other, not as floating heads, but as embodied persons with rich histories and experiences that we can all learn from and with. These embodied practices make space for teaching and learning across difference that aid in the cognitive and affective flourishing for all people. Womanish modes of play aid in creating clearing spaces that encourage brave storytelling, re-storying, and even resisting. When we can freely practice embodied aesthetic experiences and express ourselves culturally then we are able to make meaning and have our being according to our own stories and realities, and to embrace ourselves and embody God's love for ourselves and others. When we begin to value these other embodied selves, we can engage culture and community in new critically conscious ways that will enkindle the world and disrupt these systems that allow various oppressions and injustices to occur within our theological schools. Womanish modes of play can aid in igniting this type of transformative learning, teaching, and knowing that is both liberating and holistic.

How?

Having the knowledge that this work is needed and actually doing the work are very different. There is the question of how. How does one begin to train, prepare, and form persons in this approach? How does one mix womanish modes of play into pedagogy? How does one promote and prepare the conversation and have theological education faculty see the value in becoming more embodied and imaginative? I believe the how begins with vulnerability in asking deliberate questions, persists with critical consciousness and mutuality, and becomes transformative through creative and collaborative imagination and fun.

Asking deliberate questions and being vulnerable are not easy tasks. They involve the difficult work of thinking through one's own history, biases, and understandings and asking why they are what they are, how they were formed that way, and why. This involves self-reflection and an interrogation of self to move forward with critical awareness and consciousness. This includes taking the time to learn one's history in regard to racial and ethnic makeup, family ties and connections, geography, cultural realities, economic realities, and religious affiliations within the larger world. Once a person learns their history they can assess and evaluate how they have been affected by the dominant narrative and how that history impacts their own understanding and perspective of the world. As a religious educator, it is vital that this work is done prior to engaging the embodied practices with students. I am not saying you need to have it all figured out, as we are all at various places in this journey, but I am saying we need to at least start the process before we ask others to engage in it. We must do the work ourselves to be prepared to walk others through it. We should understand and be able to express the vulnerability and deliberate questioning required before asking it of others.

Once we have been vulnerable enough to interrogate our own history, understandings, and worldviews we can begin to become critically aware of our own situatedness in the world and truly begin to embrace ourselves and we who are. Once we do that, we can begin to engage our culture and community. This might look like traveling and gaining exposure and perspective or taking time to listen and share stories and narratives. Once we are able to become critically conscious and aware we can then begin to see and understand how mutuality aids in the creation of clearing space through allowing all persons to feel equally important. Valuing each person's presence, voice, and experience is vital for womanish modes of play. If one doesn't feel valued or that their body matters, engaging and being vulnerable can be very difficult. Persons must feel equally heard and valued to feel brave and courageous enough to then be vulnerable and engage in embodied playful practices.

When we vulnerably ask deliberate questions, become critically aware enough to practice mutuality, there is then clearing space for creative and collaborative imagination and fun as we embody God's creative love for ourselves leading us to enkindle the world. Engaging in embodied learning, and specifically womanish modes of play, involves creativity, imagination, and fun. We must be open to play. This might mean creating a daily play practice or engaging in activities that we did when we were a child in order to reengage our playful and imaginative nature. Coloring in a coloring book, playing with Play-Doh, taking a nature walk, or using Legos to make something are just a few ways to spark creativity and imagination. One helpful thing to imagine or envision would be where we would like to be or what we would like to see happening in our classrooms. Imagining, visioning, and hoping can aid us in working toward making that vision a reality. For example, if we imagine a more inclusive classroom space, we might begin reading more global voices so we can place them on our syllabi. This might mean creating a clearing space in our classroom by having a set aside time for sharing stories and cultivating relationships at the beginning. This might mean being vulnerable enough to be silly and surprise ourselves by dancing, singing, or playing a board game together. It is in the creativity that transformation and liberation become possible.

For some, this might mean bringing in a consulting group to facilitate and aid in the teaching and implementation of this work within the institution, the faculty or ministers, and the curriculum. For others, this might mean working through these womanish modes of play with faculty and ministers first, until they are able to see and understand its transformative impact. While this method or approach is not going to work for everyone, I do believe it can be effective in educating in faith and teaching and learning across differences and therefore is worth trying because our students are worth it. It will be important for each person in trying it to develop their own "play" approach according to their own comfort and ability levels. In order for this work to be effective it must begin with authenticity and vulnerability.

Who?

Theological education has the unique opportunity to be prophetic in highlighting the educative potential of womanish modes of play as they encompass the whole person. As theologians we care not only about education, but about educating the whole person in the love and justice of God. We take seriously the weight of sin, grace, and forgiveness; therefore when violations of personhood are not only committed, but committed in our classrooms, these issues compound making it difficult to see the love and grace of our Creator. When we allow our classrooms to be sites for acts of aggression, both micro and macro, lack of cultural awareness and inclusion, and limited critical reflection, dialogue, and consciousness, we are perpetuating systems of domination, supremacy, violence, and the fantastic hegemonic imagination. We must no longer allow these acts to go unchallenged, and to offer something in its place.

As theological educators we are all called to a mission of creating spaces to learn, grow, and explore that which our students feel called to. If the spaces we create cause unnecessary hurt and harm, then we are not effectively carrying out the mission we have been entrusted with by God. Embodied learning offers an opportunity for reconciliation of the mind and body. Womanish modes of play encourage and uplift the power of the individual voice to embrace self and story and the need to embody and share God's love. Womanish modes of play recognize the importance of cultural and communal engagement and support and the courage to set the world on fire through resisting and challenging oppression and injustice. Theological education has not only a wonderful opportunity but a responsibility to be trailblazers in this area of teaching and learning for and to the whole person through embodied practices such as womanish modes of play.

It is with all of this in mind that I offer up the rope of womanism and specifically womanish modes of play as one of many pedagogical tools that provides access to the Christian story while welcoming fun and liberative new paths for re-storying. With intentionality, a womanist pedagogy of play can be incorporated in any classroom. While this may be new and different for some, I believe in order for change to happen things must be different and disruptive. Womanish modes of play can be a starting point not just for Black women, but for all people, especially religious educators, to be bold, audacious . . . womanish in the classroom. Not only does it invite courageous behavior but allows dreaming and risking in a lower-stakes environment, in preparation for times of greater risk. In this context, womanish modes of play become prophetic and liberative practices that can remake classrooms into more holistic, transformative, and fun spaces. We can use these playful practices to critically reflect, deliberately question, and creatively and collaboratively imagine in order to live into an emancipatory hope through these embodied and liberating practices. Womanish modes of play can reshape how we learn and teach across differences for the just flourishing of all persons, as we are all made in the image and likeness of God. So, let's begin to do double Dutch together, rather than jump rope alone.

Go ahead . . . jump!

Acknowledgments

I would like to acknowledge several people who helped make this book a reality. Thank you to Dr. Evelyn Parker for believing in me and this work enough to write such an inspiring foreword. Thank you to my bestie and weekly writing partner, Dr. Jessica Young Brown. Thank you to the best childcare specialist, Ms. Dy'mon Hickman of Heaven's Knowledge Learning. I cannot offer enough thanks to Rev. Dr. Melanie Jones-Quarles and The Katie Geneva Cannon Center for Womanist Leadership for asking me to bring the Womanist Play Pedagogy class and of course the wonderful students at Union Presbyterian Seminary for testing this work out—Allison Aylor, Alex Bailey, Beth Bailey, Greta Britt, Juliette Davis, Stacy Deyerle, Ayesha Edwards, Donna Graves, Olivia Haynes Ansari, Daphne Hill, David McDowell, Janet Northern, Lesley Peace, Cris Rivera, Nicole Thompson, Shea Watts, Kristi Yeatman, and Thom Zahler.

Much of this work and research started and is inspired by my dissertation. It has been an experience of play and joy to reimagine, re-create, and expand that work into the book you have just read.

Lastly, thank you to all my family. To my spouse, children, parents, siblings, nieces, nephews, aunties, uncles, cousins, and in-laws, I love you all and am grateful to have such an amazing support system. I appreciate every one of you. I am because you are, and this book would not be made flesh in the world without all of you. I love and thank you all.

Bibliography

Berryman, Jerome. *Becoming Like a Child: The Curiosity of Maturity beyond the Norm.* New York: Church, 2017.

——. *Godly Play: An Imaginative Approach to Religious Education.* Minneapolis: Augsburg Fortress, 1991.

Black Women Oral History Project. *See* Stokes, Olivia Pearl.

Broer, Marion R. *An Introduction to Kinesiology.* Hoboken, NJ: Prentice-Hall, 1968.

Brown, Stuart. *Play: How It Shapes the Brain, Opens the Imagination, and Invigorates the Soul.* New York: Penguin Group, 2009.

Cannon, Katie Geneva. *Katie's Canon: Womanism and the Soul of the Black Community.* New York: Continuum, 1995.

Copeland, M. Shawn. *Enfleshing Freedom: Body, Race, and Being.* Minneapolis: Fortress, 2010.

Csikszentmihalyi, Mihaly. "Play and Intrinsic Rewards." *Journal of Humanistic Psychology* 15, no. 3 (July 1975): 41–63.

Douglas, Kelly Brown. *Stand Your Ground: Black Bodies and the Justice of God.* New York: Orbis Books, 2005.

Du Bois, W. E. B. *The Souls of Black Folk.* 100th anniversary ed. New York: Signet Classic, 1995.

Eberle, Scott G. "The Elements of Play." *Journal of Play* 6 no. 2 (2014): 214–33.

Floyd-Thomas, Stacey M. "Cultivating a Pedagogy of Possibility: A Womanist Christian Social Ethicist's Teaching Philosophy." Teaching philosophy while associate professor of ethics and director of Black church studies at Brite Divinity School in Fort Worth, TX.

——. *Mining the Motherlode: Methods in Womanist Ethics*. Cleveland: Pilgrim, 2006.

Floyd-Thomas, Stacey M., ed. *Deeper Shades of Purple: Womanism in Religion and Society*. New York: New York University Press, 2006.

Freire, Paolo. *Pedagogy of the Oppressed*. Translated by Myra Bergman Ramos. New York: Continuum, 2005.

Gadamer, Hans-Georg. *Truth and Method*. New York: Continuum, 1975.

Garcia-Rivera, Alejandro. *The Community of the Beautiful: A Theological Aesthetics*. Collegeville: Liturgical Press, 1999.

Gates, Henry Louis, Jr. *The Signifying Monkey: A Theory of African-American Literary Criticism*. New York: Oxford University Press, 1988.

Gilkes, Cheryl Townsend. *If It Wasn't for the Women*. New York: Orbis Books, 2001.

Glynn, Mary Ann, and Jane Webster. "The Adult Playfulness Scale: An Initial Assessment." *Psychological Reports* 71, no. 1 (August 1992): 83–103.

Goto, Courtney. *The Grace of Playing: Pedagogies for Leaning into God's New Creation*. Eugene, OR: Pickwick, 2016.

Guthrie, Steven R. *Creator Spirit: The Holy Spirit and the Art of Becoming Human*. Grand Rapids: Baker Academic, 2011.

Hamman, Jaco J. *A Play-Full Life: Slowing Down and Seeking Peace*. Cleveland: Pilgrim, 201.

Harvey, Lincoln. *A Brief Theology of Sport*. London: SCM, 2014.

Hersey, Tricia. *Rest Is Resistance: A Manifesto*. New York: Little, Brown Spark, 2022.

Hodge, Letitia. *My Pledge of Allegiance to Me*. 2004. http://www.tribute toblackwomen.com/poems/pledge.htm.

hooks, bell. *Teaching Critical Thinking: Practical Wisdom*. New York: Routledge, 2010.

——. *Teaching to Transgress: Education as the Practice of Freedom*. New York: Routledge, 1994.

Huizinga, Johan. *Homo Ludens: A Study of the Play Element in Culture*. Boston: Beacon, 1950.

Isasi-Diaz, Ada Maria. "Kin-dom of God: A *Mujerista* Proposal." In *In Our*

Own Voices: Latino/a Renditions of Theology, edited by Benjamín Valentín, 171–90. Maryknoll, NY: Orbis Books, 2010.

———. *Mujerista Theology: A Theology for the Twenty-First Century*. Maryknoll, NY: Orbis Books, 1996.

Jennings, Willie James. *The Christian Imagination: Theology and the Origins of Race*. New Haven: Yale University Press, 2010.

Jensen, Eric. *Teaching with the Brain in Mind*. 2nd ed. Alexandria, VA: Association for Supervision and Curriculum Development, 2005.

Kazanjian, David. *The Colonizing Trick: National Culture and Imperial Citizenship in Early America*. Minneapolis: University of Minnesota Press, 2003.

Kemp, G., M. Smith, B. DeKoven, and J. Segal. "Play, Creativity, and Lifelong Learning: Why Play Matters for Both Kids and Adults." 2011. (Updated May 2009.) http://helpguide.org/life/creative_play_fun_games.htm (Accessed November 5, 2015).

Kirk-Duggan, Cheryl A. "Signifying Love and Embodied Relationality: Toward a Womanist Theological Anthropology." In *Womanist and Black Feminist Responses to Tyler Perry's Productions*, edited by LeRhonda S. Manigault-Bryant, Tamura A. Lomax, and Carol B. Duncan, 41–56. New York: Palgrave Macmillan, 2014.

Kolb, Alice Y., and David A. Kolb. "Learning to Play, Playing to Learn. A Case Study of a Ludic Learning Space." *Journal of Organizational Change Management* 23, no. 1 (2010): 26–50.

Kwok Pui-lan. *Postcolonial Imagination and Feminist Theology*. Louisville: Westminster John Knox, 2005.

LaCugna, Catherine Mowry. *God for Us: The Trinity and Christian Life*. New York: HarperOne, 1991.

Lengel, Traci, and Mike Kuczala. *The Kinesthetic Classroom: Teaching and Learning through Movement*. Thousand Oaks, CA: Corwin, 2010.

Lockhart, Lakisha. "Enfleshing Catechesis through Embodied Space." In *Together Along the Way: Conversations inspired by the Directory for Catechesis*, edited by Hosffman Ospino and Theresa O'Keefe. N.p.: Crossroad, 2021.

Long, Charles H. *Significations: Signs, Symbols, and Images in the Interpretation of Religion*. Aurora, CO: Davies Group, 1995.

Lorde, Audre. *Sister Outsider: Essays and Speeches*. New York: Crossing, 1984.

McFague, Sallie. *Metaphorical Theology: Models of God in Religious Language*. Philadelphia: Fortress, 1982.

Mitchem, Stephanie Y. *Introducing Womanist Theology*. New York: Orbis Books, 2002.

Morrison, Toni. *Beloved*. New York: Knopf, 1987.

Namulundah, Florence. *bell hooks' Engaged Pedagogy: A Transgressive Education for Critical Consciousness*. London: Bergin & Garvey, 1998.

National Center for Education Statistics. (2023). Characteristics of Postsecondary Faculty. *Condition of Education*. US Department of Education, Institute of Education Sciences. November 2023, from https://nces.ed.gov/programs/coe/indicator/csc. Table 315.20

National Center for Education Statistics. (2022). Undergraduate Enrollment. *Condition of Education*. US Department of Education, Institute of Education Sciences. Retrieved June 16, 2023, from https://nces.ed.gov/programs/coe/indicator/cha. Table 306.10.

Patterson, Marilyn Nikimaa. *Every Body Can Learn: Engaging the Bodily-Kinesthetic Intelligence in the Everyday Classroom*. Tucson, AZ: Zephyr Press, 1997.

Proyer, René T., and Willibald Ruch. "The Virtuousness of Adult Playfulness." *Psychology of Well-Being: Theory, Research and Practice* 1, no. 4 (2011): 1–12.

Riggs, Marcia Y. *Awake, Arise, and Act: A Womanist Call for Black Liberation*. Cleveland: Pilgrim, 1994.

Shange, Ntozake. *For Colored Girls Who Have Considered Suicide When the Rainbow Is Enuf: A Choreopoem*. New York: Macmillan, 1977.

Sheppard, Phillis Isabella, *Self, Culture, and Others in Womanist Practical Theology*. New York: Palgrave Macmillan, 2011.

Smith, Y. Y., and M. E. Moore. "Olivia Pearl Stokes: A Living Testimony of Faith." In *Faith of Our Foremothers*, edited by B. Keely, 100–120. Louisville: Westminster John Knox, 1997.

Stockitt, Robin. *Imagination and the Playfulness of God*. Eugene, OR: Pickwick, 2011.

Stokes, Olivia Pearl. Interview by Sandra Watson, Black Women Oral History Project, September 25, 1979, Schlesinger Library, Rad-

cliffe Institute, 39. Transcript and recording at https://hollisar
chives.lib.harvard.edu/repositories/8/archival_objects/2485375.

——. "Education in the Black Church: Design for Change." In *Who Are We? The Quest for a Religious Education*, edited by John H. Wester-hoff, 218-34. Birmingham, AL: Religious Education Press, 1978.

Tanner, Kathryn. *Theories of Culture: A New Agenda for Theology.* Minneapolis: Fortress, 1997.

Thomas, Linda E. "Womanist Theology, Epistemology, and a New Anthropological Paradigm." *Cross Currents* 48, no. 4 (Summer 1998): 488-99.

Townes, Emilie M. *Womanist Ethics and the Cultural Production of Evil.* New York: Palgrave Macmillan, 2006.

Turman, Eboni Marshall. *Toward a Womanist Ethic of Incarnation: Black Bodies, the Black Church, and the Council of Chalcedon.* New York: Palgrave Macmillan, 2013.

Walker, Alice. *In Search of Our Mothers' Gardens: Womanist Prose.* New York: Harcourt, Brace, 1983.

White, Andrea C. Course description for "Theological Anthropology in Womanist Thought" class at Union Theological Seminary, Fall 2016.

Williams, Delores. *Sisters in the Wilderness: The Challenge of Womanist God-Talk.* Maryknoll, NY: Orbis Books, 1993.

Wimberly, Anne Streaty. *Soul Stories: African American Christian Education.* Nashville: Abingdon, 2005.

Winnicott, D. W. *The Maturational Processes and the Facilitating Environment: Studies in the Theory of Emotional Development.* New York: International Universities Press, 1965.

Index